The Passion and Persuasion

The Passion and Persuasion

A Biblical Deconstruction
of the Evangelical Rhetoric of the Cross

For Don + Nancy Dossett,

a wonderful couple in lifelong
service to the cause of Christ
in the world,

Elizabeth C. Gullison

Robert Hach

To order additional copies of this book, contact:
Xlibris Corporation
1-888-795-4274
www.Xlibris.com
Orders@Xlibris.com
59796

CONTENTS

PROLOGUE

The present volume is a book of theology. As such, it may have limited appeal. It is, however, a book that addresses a *theological* issue with a *rhetorical* interest. That is to say, with an interest in the effect of theology – God-talk[1] – on human thinking and feeling and acting.[2] As such, it may have broader appeal in that the effect of theology on the thinking, feeling and acting not only of many Americans but also of many non-Americans continues to have a significant impact on – and, in the case of Islamic fundamentalism, to pose a significant threat to – American society.

The specific theological issue that the present volume addresses is that of the meaning of the crucifixion of Jesus. Why this is even an issue may not be at all obvious.

The meaning of Jesus' crucifixion – or, in the language of traditional theology, *the atonement* – was a theological issue at various points in the history of Christianity but seems to have long since been settled. The reason for this may be that only one branch of organized Christianity continues

---

[1] The term *theology* comes from the Greek, *theos*, the Greek term for God, and *logos*, usually rendered "word," in its original sense combining both the ideas of reason and persuasion: reasonably persuasive talk about God.

[2] The traditional definition of *rhetoric* is *the art of persuasion*, as in the study of persuasion as a methodology: what works in terms of the use of language to produce desirable belief and, through belief, desirable behavior. The term *rhetoric* in popular usage has long since connoted a verbal sleight of hand designed to win votes or sell products. From an academic standpoint, however, *rhetoric* has gradually come to signify, more generally, the way language works on the human mind, not only consciously but unconsciously, not only individually but also collectively.

to place the atonement front and center, at the heart of its message, that branch being what is commonly called *evangelical Christianity*.[3] And the evangelical doctrine of the atonement – what I will term *the evangelical rhetoric of the cross* – is central to its identity as "the Church," and to the sense of individual evangelical Christians that they are "saved," as in "right with God" and "Heaven-bound" when they die. As far as evangelical Christianity is concerned, its rhetoric of the cross is not considered a matter of biblical interpretation (though this doctrine was not the prevailing understanding of the atonement for the first thousand years of Christian history) but a doctrine so unequivocally and dogmatically set forth by the Bible that to fail to believe it is to be considered an unbeliever, lost in sin and, therefore, without hope.

My intention is to unsettle the evangelical rhetoric of the cross. First, I wish to show that it squares neither with a New Testament (NT) understanding nor with a logical understanding of the NT words. (While it may seem to positivists illogical on its face, theology is nothing if not the attempt to talk logically about God.) Second, I hope to show that the evangelical rhetoric of the cross enshrines and projects an image of "God," the spirit of which is embodied by the collective force of evangelical Christianity in America, that stands in radical opposition to the biblical message and its God.

I

The evangelical doctrine of the atonement was officially formulated in the middle ages, becoming the authorized doctrine of Catholic, and subsequently of Protestant, Christianity. Together with the doctrine of the Trinity, the evangelical rhetoric of the cross is the evangelical "gospel," which is continually propagated by evangelicals from their pulpits, through their books, on their radio and television programs, and via the World Wide Web, as well as person-to-person, throughout the world on a daily basis.

In sum, the evangelical rhetoric of the cross is that God-the-Son died for sinners to pay God-the-Father to forgive sinners so that God-the-Holy-Spirit

---

[3]   As far as Catholic and liberal Protestant Christianity are concerned, the meaning of the atonement is not nearly as important as its role as a symbol linking the Church of the present to its past, securing its approved status in the ecclesiastical tradition.

could live within sinners, making them children of God and giving them eternal life. (This doctrine of the atonement is thus inseparable from the doctrine of the Trinity.) The payment was allegedly demanded by God the Father because his justice requires that his law be perfectly obeyed, and that every transgression of his law be paid for by the punishment of eternal condemnation. The payment was not only demanded but also provided by the Father in the substitutionary person of the Son by means of the blood which the Son shed on the cross. The payment made by God-the-Son allows God-the-Father *to justify and, therefore, forgive sinners*, who receive the indwelling presence of the Father and the Son in the Person of God-the-Holy-Spirit.

Why should thoughtful Christians question the evangelical rhetoric of the cross? (And why should others who have, perhaps, rejected biblical faith because they have been unable to accept this doctrine question whether it is, in fact, taught by the NT writers?) After all, this doctrine of the atonement has been instrumental to the hope of "eternal life" for members of "the Church" for at least the last thousand years (there having been no fixed meaning of the atonement during the first thousand years of Christianity). In that this doctrine of the atonement is the evangelical gospel, the "good news" that evangelists announce to prospective believers – after having confronted them with the bad news of their standing as condemned sinners in the eyes of a just God – to question its truth would seem to shake the very foundation of the historic Christian faith.

On the other hand, the evangelical rhetoric of the cross has never been a matter of consensus on the part of NT interpreters. For the first thousand years of the Christian tradition, no strictly orthodox doctrine of the atonement was recognized by "the Church." Thereafter, following the establishment of the medieval theologian Anselm of Canterbury's interpretation of the atonement – set forth in his book, *Cur Deus Homo* (in English, *Why the God Man?*) – as the orthodox doctrine of Christianity, periodic challenges were presented (albeit by minority voices in the Christian tradition). Nevertheless, Anselm's interpretation (also called by scholars the Latin, or legal, theory) of the atonement prevailed to the extent that today, it is revered by evangelical Christians as if it had sprung fully grown from the pages of scripture. And this despite the fact that it is nowhere spelled out by the NT writers, making it a matter of inference, at best merely implicit, as opposed to an explicit NT teaching (a fact that is common to both this doctrine of the atonement *and* the doctrine of the Trinity).

Not only do the NT writers not spell out the evangelical doctrine of the atonement, but NT scholarship has also increasingly concluded that they do not spell out any specific interpretation. Writes Gerard Sloyin,

> One needs to ask . . . whether the New Testament writers provide anything like a full-blown theory of human atonement or reconciliation by the shedding of Christ's blood. The answer seems to be no. There is only the tradition, already in place when Paul becomes a believer in the risen Lord, "that Christ died for our sins" (1 Cor. 15:3) [and that] "All who believe are justified [i.e., acquitted] freely by God's grace through the redemption in Christ Jesus, whom God set forth as a means of expiation in his blood, through faith, to demonstrate God's righteousness, because in the divine forbearance God had let the sins committed in the past go unpunished to demonstrate his righteousness in the present, that God might be righteous and justify anyone who believes in Jesus" (Rom. 3:24-26).[i]

To be sure, Paul and the other NT writers used the metaphors of *justification*, *redemption*, *propitiation*, *reconciliation*, and *ransom* to describe the theological effect of Jesus' crucifixion, but they do not explain specifically how the shedding of Jesus' blood accomplished that effect. (As I hope to show, the NT writers assumed certain understandings that made specific explanations unnecessary, understandings however that could no longer be assumed once the post-apostolic Christian leadership shifted from Jewish to Gentile hands.) As a result, any theory of the atonement based on the NT data is a matter of inference. And if so, an understanding of the atonement should be subject to persuasive discourse regarding the meaning of the relevant NT texts, rather than imposed on professing Christians by the keepers of the evangelical faith.[4]

Nevertheless, though Anselm's theory of the atonement only gradually emerged as the unquestioned doctrine of Christianity, it has become so enshrined in evangelical Christian faith – central as it is to the very "gospel"

---

[4]   The fact that the NT writers do not "provide anything like a full-blown theory of" the atonement does not mean, however, that a theory of the atonement cannot be constructed that is consistent with the NT data, and both logically and theologically satisfying, as I hope to show.

of evangelicalism – that to question its truth seems to constitute questioning the truth of the Bible itself. Nevertheless, besides the fact that it did not always hold the sacrosanct place in the Christian tradition that it does now, another compelling reason exists for reexamining the meaning of the atonement of Christ.

II

Arguably, the chief problem with the evangelical rhetoric of the cross is that *it excludes the possibility of forgiveness*. In effect, this doctrine renders its God unable to forgive. How so?

Forgiveness is, literally, the cancellation of an *unpaid* debt. Which is to say that *forgiveness is the alternative to demanding payment of a debt*. One can demand payment of a debt and, subsequently, cancel the debt upon payment, *or* one can cancel the debt without payment. One cannot do both. Forgiveness can only be the latter.

The evangelical rhetoric of the cross asserts that God forgives sinners *because* Jesus paid their debt of sin. Which is to say that God cancelled *not* an unpaid debt but a debt which was paid in full. But the *payment* of the debt logically eliminates the need, or the possibility, of the *forgiveness* of the debt.

The Trinitarian formulation that God (in the Person of the Son) paid God (in the Person of the Father) the debt does not mitigate the contradictory notion that the debt had to be paid to enable God to forgive. To say that the debt of sin had to be *paid* to enable God to *forgive* the debt is to utter nonsense (a piece of nonsense that the NT writers themselves never put forth.) *A debt that has been paid can no longer be forgiven.*

Forgiveness is an economic metaphor, which includes the financial elements of debt and payment. If one is owed a hundred dollars by another, one can cancel the debt, freeing the other from the obligation to pay it. The forgiven debtor may then, figuratively speaking, owe a debt of gratitude, but he or she no longer owes a financial debt. This is forgiveness: the debt goes unpaid and is deliberately forgotten. If a third party pays the debt, however, the one who is owed cancels the debt because it has been paid. This is not forgiveness. Neither is it forgiveness to say that one who is owed one hundred dollars forgives the debt by paying oneself one hundred dollars – which roughly corresponds to the Trinitarian claim that God-the-Son paid the debt of sin to God-the-Father. This is, at best, to assert a redundancy. In reality, no payment is made when the debt is cancelled by the one to whom it is owed. *The ideas of forgiveness and payment are mutually exclusive.*

When interpersonal relations are moral rather than financial, the same reasoning must apply if the word "forgiveness" is to be used in a meaningful way. When one is wronged morally by another and is, therefore, owed a kind of moral debt, one cannot take vengeance – which is the appropriate word for making the offender pay – on a third party, much less on oneself (or a part of oneself) instead of on the wrong-doer, and then call it "forgiveness." Payment and forgiveness are still mutually exclusive. One who took vengeance on oneself rather than on the offender would be considered neither forgiving nor just; instead, one would be considered insane. Unless, that is, one were the evangelical God, who apparently doesn't play by the same rules.

III

At issue in this apparent conundrum is the NT concept of *justification*. The evangelical notion is that God could only *justifiably* forgive sinners if their sins were paid for. That is to say, *forgiveness must somehow be reconciled to legal justice* before forgiveness can be extended. The problem is that it is not within the province of legal justice to forgive transgressions of law. Legal justice rewards obedience and punishes disobedience; its function does not include, and in fact precludes, forgiving disobedience. Therefore, if God is to be legally *just*, sin – defined as disobedience to God's law – must be punished *rather than* forgiven. Which is to say that *a God whose justice is legal cannot forgive.*

The evangelical rhetoric of the cross addresses this issue by proposing a "tension" between *justice* and *mercy* in the very being of God. God is *just* and, therefore, must punish transgressions of his law; at the same time, God is *merciful* and, therefore, wishes to forgive transgressions of his law.

Note the priority of justice over mercy in this theological construct: the problem of forgiveness is created by the *already-existing* justice of God. God's mercy cannot be expressed in the form of forgiveness *until after* justice has been satisfied, making justice more central, more integral, than mercy to the being of the evangelical God. Justice is, in this view, an *attribute* of God whereas mercy is, at most, a secondary attribute that God can manifest *only after his justice has been satisfied* (in the sense of being pacified or neutralized) by a suitable payment. This accords with the common evangelical notion of the *Decalogue* (i.e., the Ten Commandments) as a kind of blueprint of

God's nature. In this view, God is *ontologically* – that is, at the core of his very being – a God of law. (Notwithstanding the NT writers' claim that "God is love" [1 John 4:8] and the absence of any NT claim that God *is* law.)

The blood of Christ, then, is alleged by the evangelical doctrine to *resolve the tension between God's justice and God's mercy*, allowing God to both uphold his justice and to extend his mercy.

Nevertheless, if plain language is to mean what it says, one (even God) cannot both justify *and* forgive – that is, if *to justify* means to reward for obedience. One could conceivably transfer the reward for obedience from the one who obeyed (in this case, Jesus) to another or others (in this case, sinners), as indeed the evangelical rhetoric of the cross claims that God did by transferring the legal righteousness that Jesus earned (by obeying the law) to sinners. And one could conceivably accept the payment of one for another's debt, which the evangelical doctrine also claims that God did by accepting Jesus' death in lieu of the death (albeit understood as the unending conscious torment in Hell) of sinners. *But this is not forgiveness.* For forgiveness can have nothing to do with earning or paying in that it can only be freely given.

Once again, one cannot demand and accept payment of a debt *and then* cancel the debt *as if it had not been paid.*

That is, unless when the NT Jesus said, "What is impossible with men is possible with God" (Luke 18:27), he included the logic-defying ability to "have his cake and eat it too." For Christians who feel no need to understand what they believe, logical contradictions do not pose a problem for their faith. In fact, many seem to believe that since God cannot be contained within logical systems of thought, logic – in the sense of reasoning – has no place in the realm of the spirit.

Be that as it may, the evangelical rhetoric of the cross is nothing if not an attempt to *logically* understand the theo*logical* necessity for Jesus' death on the cross. That it contradicts logic in its portrayal of God's forgiveness is a reason not to question whether logical reasoning has a place in Christian faith – *theology* is, after all, the application of *logos* (the ancient Greek word for the reasoning power of language) to the question of *theos* (the ancient Greek word for God). Instead, the fact that the evangelical doctrine makes *logical nonsense* is a reason to question whether it is the most reasonable interpretation of the NT language of the atonement.

Even more so in that the product of this logical contradiction is a theological monstrosity: a "God" at odds with himself, torn between *justice* and *mercy* – between *law* and *love*, between *wrath* and *grace* – who can only reconcile himself to himself, and to his world, by an act of sadistic violence. A God who could only resolve the tension within himself and achieve integrity by engineering the gruesome death by torture of his only Son.

The notion that sinners are the beneficiaries of this tortured logic is questionable at best. Despite the theological gymnastics that have gone into manufacturing the evangelical doctrine of the atonement, the *logical* and, therefore, *theological* product is a God who is unable to extend authentic forgiveness. For a "forgiveness" that must be paid for is no forgiveness at all.

The word "forgiveness" is, of course, employed by Christians publicly in sermons and lessons, and privately in counseling sessions and other interactions all over the world. Nevertheless, the fact that the word cannot be employed by evangelical Christians apart from the virtually unquestioned assumption that it is a forgiveness for which God had to be paid (albeit paid by himself) can only undermine its persuasive power, however unconsciously. For, even unconsciously, *people know that real forgiveness is free.* (Which may explain why so many Christians live under the burden of a religious guilt that makes them vulnerable to both religious and secular manipulation.)

Forgiveness, of course, must be accepted, which means both acknowledging the need for it and experiencing its reconciling effects on the relationship between the forgiver and the forgiven. But *the acceptance of forgiveness is built on the assumption that it has been freely given.*

IV

None of the foregoing critique of the evangelical rhetoric of the cross is intended to cast doubt on the biblical message that the apostle Paul called "the word of the cross" (1 Cor. 1:18). Its purpose is, rather, to call into question the dubious interpretation that is the unquestioned evangelical dogma regarding the atonement of Christ.

The question is not, then, whether or not Jesus died for sins, nor even if Jesus' death paid for sins. The question is, rather, how the NT language of atonement should be understood. What truth does Jesus' death on the cross reveal about God? And about how to relate to God?

Gustav Aulen, in his seminal volume *Christus Victor: An Historical Study of the Three Main Types of the Idea of Atonement,* explains the significance of the atonement of Christ – and, thus, of how the atonement of Christ is understood – for faith in God:

> The subject of the Atonement is absolutely central in Christian theology; and it is directly related to that of the nature of God. Each and every interpretation of the Atonement is most closely connected with some conception of the essential meaning of Christianity, and reflects some conception of the Divine nature. Indeed, it is in some conception of the nature of God that every doctrine of the Atonement has its ultimate ground.[ii]

In short, then, what does "the word of the cross," understood in NT terms, persuade its hearers to believe about God and, accordingly, about how to relate to God? And what could be more central and crucial to faith than the question of how to relate to God?

It is undeniable that the NT writers claim that, through the agency of Jesus' death on the cross, God provided both payment for sins *and* forgiveness of sins. How this can be, given that forgiveness is the cancellation of an unpaid debt, is a paradox that must be addressed by any theory of the atonement that would do justice to the NT "word of the cross." What follows is an attempt both to deconstruct the evangelical rhetoric of the cross and to offer an alternative that does rhetorical justice to the biblical message and its God.

Endnotes

i. Gerard S. Sloyin, *The Crucifixion of Jesus: History, Myth, Faith* (Minneapolis: Fortune Press, 1995), 100.

ii. Gustav Aulen, *Christus Victor: An Historical Study of the Three Main Types of the Idea of Atonement* (New York: MacMillan, 1969), 12-13.

CHAPTER 1

The Question of Justice

"For I am not ashamed of the gospel, for . . . in it the righteousness[1] of God is revealed from faith for faith, as it is written, 'The righteous[2] shall live by faith'" (Rom. 1:16, 17).

"But now the righteousness of God has been manifested apart from the law . . ." (Rom. 3:21).

Perhaps the most appalling feature of the evangelical rhetoric of the cross is its claim that God's *justice* (or, synonymously, his *righteousness*) requires him to demand payment for sins.

This is an insoluble problem in regard to forgiveness because if God must demand payment for sins – even if God makes the payment himself – God cannot forgive. As long as forgiveness means *the cancellation of an unpaid debt*, then one (even God) cannot demand and accept payment for the debt *and* forgive the debt. To cancel a debt because it has been paid (even if, however nonsensically, by oneself) obviously excludes the possibility of cancelling an *unpaid* debt.

Why, then, did the NT writers seem to have no apparent difficulty claiming both that God is just and that God forgives sins? Not only so, but the NT writers went so far as to claim that God forgives sins *because* he is

---

[1]   The NT Greek word, *dikaiosune*, can be translated either "righteousness" or "justice."

[2]   The NT Greek word, *dikaios*, can be translated either "righteous" or "just."

Unless He did not pay the whole thing

"just": "If we confess our sins, he is faithful and just to forgive us our sins and to cleanse us from all unrighteousness" (1 John 1:9).

The evangelical argument is that God is "just to forgive" *only because the demand of his justice for payment has been satisfied by Jesus' death on the cross*. Therefore, God can now *justifiably* forgive, based on the application of Jesus' payment to sinners. This assumes, of course, that forgiveness can only be justified – can only be right – if it is paid for. Forgiveness, accordingly, cannot be freely given.

I have so argued re: Mt 6:12, 14-15

The main problem with this argument is that *if forgiveness can only be justified if the debt of sin is paid, then forgiveness cannot be justified at all*. This is the case because forgiveness – the cancellation of *an unpaid debt* – is not forgiveness *unless it is freely given*.

The NT writers, however, seem to have been unaware of any difficulty in reconciling the justice and the mercy of God. Which is to say that *forgiveness does not have to be justified* in any legal sense as far as they were concerned. While the function of legal justice is to reward and punish, as opposed to providing forgiveness, the function of the biblical God's justice includes forgiving sinners. To repeat, for the NT writers, God forgives *because* he is just.

Forgiveness, mercy, and grace are as integral to the biblical God as is justice. Not only so, but for the biblical writers God's forgiveness-mercy-and-grace are an expression of God's justice, which is another name for God's love.

But what kind of justice is equivalent to love?

Equivalents?

I

Historically speaking, Western civilization is largely the product of two cultural traditions: the Judeo-Christian tradition and the Greco-Roman tradition. The former is generally identified with Western religion and the latter with Western politics, philosophy and education. The secular Western tendency to segregate religious faith from political, educational and philosophical discourse, however, has disguised the extent to which the Judeo-Christian religious tradition is less a distinct tradition than a corollary of the Greco-Roman political-educational-philosophical tradition. In other words, quite early on, the Greco-Roman tradition became the filter through which the Judeo-Christian tradition was strained, to the extent that the prophetic understanding of God that originally set both Jews and *but provided a token the Father accepted in lieu.*

Christians apart from the Greco-Roman world was soon lost, replaced by Greek philosophical and Roman legal concepts.

Which is to say that what Americans call the "Judeo-Christian tradition" is, in historical fact, a tradition that was reformulated by both the languages (i.e., Greek and Latin) and the ideologies (philosophical and political) of the Greco-Roman world in which Christianity emerged, and the Greco-Roman tradition has carried both Judaism and Christianity into the contemporary world.

While the NT writers expressed their thoughts *in* the Greek language, they addressed their thoughts *to* the Roman world (Greek being the international language of the Roman Empire). Nevertheless, the thought world of the NT writers was *not* shaped and structured by the *Greek philosophy* or *Roman law* which had already shaped and structured the cultural education, and therefore the thought world, of their Gentile readers. Instead, the concepts of the NT writers came from *Hebrew prophecy*. The Hebrew prophets' ideas about God informed what Christians now call the Old Testament (OT), the Hebrew scriptures from which the NT writers' ideas about God were drawn. Accordingly, *the NT writers expressed Hebrew thoughts in Greek words to a Roman world.* In the process, the Hebrew prophetic tradition could not help but clash with – and be altered by – the Greek philosophical and Roman legal traditions that permeated the education and culture of the Gentile subjects of the Roman Empire.

This clash was, at its root, ideological, occurring in and between minds, first, when the NT message was heard, and later when the NT writings were read, by Gentiles. NT faith required, for Gentiles, a virtual *re-education* that broke the cultural grip of the Greek and Roman religious mythology out of which the Greek philosophical and Roman legal traditions arose.

That this re-educational process was as successful as it was in the first century – judging by the spread of the NT message throughout the Roman Empire – is made more remarkable by the fact that it was purely the product of persuasive discourse. Only two to three centuries later, after the Roman Empire was "Christianized" by the Emperor Constantine, could "the Church" (having already internalized Roman law organizationally and Greek philosophy ideologically) carry out a coercive program of indoctrination to impose its ecclesiastical orthodoxy on the masses.

As long as the leadership of the first-century Jesus-community was largely Jewish, then the apostolic tradition, which produced the NT writings as an extension of the Hebrew prophetic tradition, could govern believers through persuasion. After the passing of the apostolic generation, however, the center of activity shifted from Jerusalem to Rome, and from Jewish to Gentile leadership (a development which was hastened by the Roman destruction of Jerusalem in 70 C.E.). As a result, the Greco-Roman tradition became increasingly more decisive than the Hebrew tradition in the way the Gentile leaders of the Jesus-community interpreted the NT writers until, eventually, virtually all traces of the Hebrew thought world were erased from ecclesiastical orthodoxy. The apostolic tradition was increasingly reinterpreted to echo the ideological imperatives of Greek philosophy and Roman law.

The ecclesiastical concept of God's justice (or righteousness) is a prime example of the eradication of Hebrew thought from the Christian tradition. Biblical scholarship has uncovered the fact that the Hebrew concept of justice differed radically from the Roman – or Latin, or legal – concept that Western culture inherited and that became integral to the ecclesiastical doctrine of the atonement. According to Robert Brinsmead (to whose writings I am indebted for my first awareness of an alternative understanding of justice),

> The Latin concept of justice was called *justitia distributiva* (distributive justice). This meant giving every man exactly what he deserves or merits. This became the standard Western idea of justice. It influenced the way the Western church read the Bible and interpreted many of the great doctrines of the Christian faith.[i]

While the Roman concept of justice is *legal* – that is, the upholding of law by rewarding obedience and punishing disobedience – the Hebrew concept of justice is of an entirely different sort, best modified by the adjective *covenantal*. The Hebrew God made covenants with his people, agreements based on promises which he made, and they agreed to believe and behave accordingly. Which is to say that *the Hebrew concept of justice consists not in the upholding of law but in the keeping of promise.*

A covenant is a relationship of promise in that one party makes a promise and another party believes the promise, creating a bond between the two that depends on *mutual faithfulness*. The one who makes the promise faithfully keeps, or fulfills, the promise, and the one who believes the promise keeps faith with the promise by acting in reliance on the promise and in assurance that the promise will be fulfilled. The Hebrew concept of *justice*, then, is the idea of *covenant faithfulness*.

Unlike legal justice, the biblical God's justice provided neither what his people *deserved* nor what they *desired*. Instead, *the covenantal justice of God provided exactly what his people needed.*

Consequently, God "is faithful and just to forgive us our sins . . ." (1 John 1:9). This text employs the literary device called *Hebrew parallelism*, according to which synonymous words or phrases appear side by side for purposes of clarity and emphasis. In this case, "faithful and just" are not two distinct attributes of God but two synonymous features of God's action in Christ which account for God's forgiveness. God forgives sins because God is "faithful," which is to say, because God is "just." By forgiving sins, then, God is being "faithful" to his promise, and in so doing, God is being "just."

But how can faithfulness to a promise be synonymous with justice?

II

Legal justice is arguably a substitute for covenantal justice. If all human beings were faithful to their promises to each other, laws that prohibit and punish dishonest behavior would be unnecessary.

The purpose of civil law is, essentially, to protect people's property rights – *property* being defined broadly to include not only one's material possessions but also one's life and labor, both physical and intellectual. (In this sense, freedom of speech and religion and other civil rights involve the exercise of one's property rights.) Membership in a society is a covenantal arrangement in that it assumes the implicit promise by each member to respect the property rights of every other member. Acts of violence or robbery or fraud or other means of depriving others of their physical, material or intellectual property are, therefore, violations of the social covenant. They are also, of course, against the law, but the point is that laws against such behavior are only necessary to the extent that faithfulness to the social covenant is tenuous or altogether absent.

Most members of democratic societies tend to show respect for the property rights of others, at least in most cases, because they have been socially conditioned to do so, with the expectation that, in turn, their own property rights will be respected. Implied in the social covenant is "the Golden Rule," according to which one treats others as one wishes to be treated. This rule, then, is an expression of covenantal justice. If all members of society were mature and responsible enough to follow that single rule, laws would be unnecessary (as, in the NT view, they will one day be in the kingdom of God). Because in most cases most members of society show, to varying degrees, respect for each other's property rights, human society is possible.

If, however, most members of society became determined to violate the social covenant by depriving their neighbors of their property rights, a declaration of martial law would be necessary. A police state is built on the assumption that legal justice is the only justice there is, that members of society cannot be trusted to keep faith with a social covenant. Police states illustrate, of course, that legal justice in the total absence of covenantal justice is no justice at all: virtually all civil and human rights are suspended in the interest of peace and safety. A society under martial law can hardly be considered a just society.

Accordingly, "the law is not laid down for the just but for the lawless . . ." (1 Tim. 1:9). Those who are "just" – that is, those who are *faithful to their promises* – do not need laws to govern their behavior because they are guided by their sense of social responsibility – an inner *law*, or principle, of faithfulness – regarding those with whom they share a covenant relationship. By comparison, "the lawless," lacking such an inner *law*, have only desires to be gratified at the expense of others. Therefore, they must be coerced with threats of punishment by a legal code to behave *as if* they possessed a sense of social responsibility.

Covenantal justice – that is, faithfulness to promise – is, therefore, the authentic version of justice. Legal justice is, accordingly, a kind of secondary and substitutionary justice, a "necessary evil" in that it is made *necessary* only by the relative absence of covenantal justice in the world. And, however necessary, legal justice *is* an evil because it must use coercion and violence to achieve its ends. Even a society's "law-abiding" members, who generally show respect for each other's property rights in the expectation that their own rights will also be respected, are sometimes tempted by – and sometimes succumb to – human passions, like envy and greed and lust, to violate the social covenant. Consequently, legal justice cannot be dispensed with in what the NT writers called "the present age of sin and death." Nevertheless, legal justice is *synthetic* rather than *authentic* justice, in that the legal justice systems of democratic nations serve as a substitute for the universal covenantal justice – the justice of love rather than of law – that the NT writers claimed awaits the coming of the kingdom of God.

III

That God's justice has always been *covenantal* rather than *legal* is made clear by the OT writers. Specifically, God's justice is displayed in his faithfulness to his promise to Abraham and in Abraham's corresponding faith in the promise and faithfulness to the God of the promise:

> You are [*YHWH*[3]], the God who chose Abram and brought him out of Ur of the Chaldeans and gave him the name Abraham. You found his heart faithful before you, and made with him the covenant to give to his offspring the land of the Canaanite, the Hittite, the Amorite, the Perizzite, the Jebusite, and the Girgashite. *And you have kept your promise, for you are righteous.* (Neh. 9:7-8)

The English words "justice" and "righteousness" are biblically synonymous in that they are translations of the same word in OT Hebrew (*sadaq*) and in NT Greek (*dikaiosune*). To declare to God, then, that "you have kept your promise, for you are righteous [i.e., just]" is to say that God's justice has been expressed in God's faithfulness to his Abrahamic promise.

Yahweh promised Abraham to give him a son (Isaac), through whom *Yahweh* would make of Abraham a great nation (Israel), through which *Yahweh* would bless all nations (see Gen. 12:1-3; 15:1-6; 18:18). And because Abraham believed God's promise, God counted Abraham's *faith as righteousness*: "And he believed [*Yahweh*], and [*Yahweh*] counted it to him as righteousness" (Gen. 15:6). Paul spelled out the idea in no uncertain terms: "Abraham believed God, and it was counted to him as righteousness" (Rom. 4:3; Gal. 3:6). Long before God gave the Mosaic law to Israel (430 years before, according to Paul in Gal. 3:17) – and, therefore, long before the possibility of confusing God's justice with a legal justice – God counted faith in his promise as "righteousness" (i.e., justice: Hebrew, *sadaq*; Greek,

---

[3]   *YHWH* is the Hebrew name for the God of Israel. *YHWH* is typically rendered "LORD" (in all capitals as opposed to "Lord," which translates the Hebrew title, *Adonai*). Sometimes vowels are added to make the name pronounceable: *Yahweh*, or alternatively, *Jahweh*, or *Jehovah*. Hereafter its appearance in OT texts will be rendered [*Yahweh*].

dikaiosune). Which is to say that the NT writers were in full agreement with their OT predecessors that God's justice had never been *legal*, a matter of law, but always *covenantal*, a matter of promise.

Yahweh's covenant with Abraham was the foundational biblical covenant, underlying the subsequent covenants after which the two major divisions of the Christian Bible are traditionally named. *The Old Testament* is about what the NT writers called the "old covenant" between *Yahweh* and Israel, the *national covenant* which administered the fulfillment of the promise to make of Abraham a great nation. *The New Testament* is about what the NT writers called the "new covenant," the *international covenant* which administers the fulfillment of the promise to bless all nations in Abraham's seed, whom Paul identified as God's *Anointed One* (in Hebrew, *meshiach*, or Messiah; in Greek, *christos*, or Christ), namely, Jesus.

The Bible, then, is essentially the story of God's *faithfulness* to his Abrahamic promise. Which is to say that the Bible was written to testify about God's *righteousness*, or *covenantal justice*. (The significance of this point is hard to overestimate: To miss it by interpreting God's justice as legal – as ecclesiastical Christianity has done throughout its history, and as evangelical Christianity continues to do – is to miss the point of the Bible itself.)

The fulfillment of God's Abrahamic promise to bless all nations includes the blessing of the forgiveness of sins, which provides believers of all nations with the assurance of God's love, that God will not count their sins against them on the day of judgment but will, instead, welcome them into his kingdom. In that God's *justice* is synonymous with God's *faithfulness* to his Abrahamic promise, the forgiveness of sins is, indeed, a demonstration of God's justice. The rhetorically manufactured tension between God's justice and God's mercy dissolves, therefore, with the understanding that God's justice is not legal but covenantal.

Many OT texts equate God's justice/righteousness (Hebrew, *sadaq*) with God's faithfulness (for examples, 1 Sam. 26:23; 1 Kgs. 3:6; Psa. 33:4-5; 36:5-6; 85:10-11; 119:138; Isa. 1:21, 26; 11:5; 16:5; Hos. 2:19-20; and Zech. 8:8). This Hebrew understanding of justice was naturally embedded in the minds of the NT writers, who saw themselves as extending the tradition of the Hebrew scriptures and who, consequently, perceived no tension between God's justice and God's mercy.

Therefore, Paul could write that in the NT message – the good news of God's fulfillment through Jesus of his Abrahamic promise to bless all nations – "the righteousness [i.e., justice] of God is revealed from faith for faith," and then quote an OT prophet to support his claim: "The righteous shall live by faith" (Rom. 1:17; Hab. 2:4). In so writing, Paul used the Greek word *dikaios* to signify not the Roman legal concept but the Hebrew covenantal concept of righteousness/justice (Hebrew, *sadaq*): " . . . now the righteousness of God has been manifested apart from the law . . ." (Rom. 3:21).

According to Paul, then, Jesus' righteousness, like Abraham's before him, was not a justification by works – a righteousness of law – but a justification by, a righteousness of, faith in God's Abrahamic promise. By proclaiming his gospel of the kingdom of God and, as a result, being put to death on the cross, Jesus exercised his own faith in God's promise to bless all nations in Abraham's Messianic seed by raising his Messiah from the dead. As a result of Jesus' righteousness of faith, God raised Jesus from the dead and exalted him to God's right hand in God's kingdom, making Jesus' righteousness of faith – including the forgiveness of sins – available to all nations through the NT message of the kingdom and grace of God.

Therefore, Paul's gospel – no different from Jesus' gospel if Paul's claim to have "received it through a revelation" from the risen Jesus himself (Gal. 1:12) is to be believed – is *the good news about God's covenantal justice*. That is, it is the announcement of God's fulfillment of his Abrahamic promise to bless all nations. This international blessing, according to the NT writers, begins with the forgiveness of sins and ends with resurrection from death to life in the kingdom of God at the end of the present age.

For Paul and the other NT writers, then, just as for the Hebrew prophets before them, *God's justice is a matter not of demand for payment but of fulfillment of promise*. Consequently, the evangelical notion that God's justice required God to demand payment for sins – and allowed him to "forgive" only because he had exacted payment from God-self in the person of Jesus – could not have entered their minds.

How, then, did the odious idea that the biblical God's nature required that he demand payment for sins enter the minds of the post-apostolic theologians who formulated the orthodox doctrine of the atonement?

IV

The earliest Christian thinker who proposed, or at least assumed, a tension between God's justice and God's mercy that prevented God from freely forgiving sins was the late-second-early-third-century Latin theologian Tertullian. His Roman background and training had instilled in his mind a concept radically different from the Hebrew concept of justice. The Roman penchant for distributive justice is illustrated in Tertullian's concept of *satisfaction*, by which he meant compensating for an offense by making a payment in the form of *penance* [ii]:

> How absurd it is to leave the penance unperformed, and yet expect forgiveness of sins! What is it but to fail to pay the price, and, nevertheless, to stretch out the hand for the benefits? The Lord has ordained that forgiveness is to be granted for this price: He wills that the remission of the penalty is to be purchased for the payment which penance makes. [iii]

Tertullian saw no contradiction in insisting that God must be paid before he would extend forgiveness. In his concern that forgiveness not leave the lives of Christians unchanged for the better, Tertullian apparently – and not surprisingly, given his Roman training – failed to see that forgiveness is not forgiveness unless it is freely given. While Tertullian himself did not apply his notion of the exchange of payment for forgiveness to the atonement, he took a decisive theological step in that direction.

Tertullian's lead was gradually followed by subsequent Latin theologians, such as Cyprian and Gregory the Great, and the concept of legal satisfaction was increasingly applied to the atonement until it reached fruition in the theory of the medieval theologian, Anselm of Canterbury:

> The Latin theory of the Atonement first appears fully developed in the *Cur Deus homo?* of Anselm; a book which has been so universally regarded as the typical expression of the Latin theory, that this theory has commonly been known as the Anselmian doctrine, and that the controversy on the Atonement has continually centred round Anselm's name. [iv]

Of course, "the Latin theory . . . has commonly been known as the Anselmian doctrine" only by Christian theologians, who have been the only ones, for all intents and purposes, to engage in "controversy" regarding the meaning of the atonement. After the middle ages, "the Anselmian doctrine" increasingly prevailed over alternative interpretations of the atonement to the extent that it eventually became a matter of orthodoxy – the evangelical gospel of "the Church" – assumed to have sprung full-grown from the pages of scripture.

Anselm's theory of the atonement is firmly rooted in Tertullian's preoccupation with penance and satisfaction. Regarding Anselm's theory, according to Aulen,

> the whole structure is built on the basis of the penitential system. Anselm's basic assumption is that the required satisfaction for transgression must be made by man, and the argument proceeds: Men are not able to make the necessary satisfaction, because they are all sinful. If men cannot do it, then God must do it. But, on the other hand, the satisfaction must be made by man, because man is guilty. The only solution is that God becomes man; this is the answer to the question *Cur Deus homo?* [Latin for, *Why the God-Man?* Anselm's classic volume about the meaning of the atonement].[v]

Sloyin, like Aulen, notes the centrality of both legal justice and "the incarnation" (i.e., God's becoming man in the person of Jesus) to Anselm's theory of the atonement:

> The only way out of the dilemma posed by the rebellion of the free human creature was by the incarnation of the Son of God, who would freely make recompense to God by offering his human life. In that way, the divine justice would be satisfied and human responsibility preserved.[vi]

Regarding the supposed tension between justice and mercy, requiring the subordination of forgiveness to "satisfaction," Aulen explains,

> We find in Anselm, as in every form of the Latin theory of the Atonement, the alternative stated: *either* a forgiveness of sins by God, which would mean that sin is not treated seriously and so would amount to a toleration of laxity, *or* satisfaction. No other possibility is regarded as conceivable. The vindication of the justice of God and His judgment on sin necessarily involves a making-good, a compensation, which satisfies the demands of justice . . . . It is an indispensable necessity that God shall receive the satisfaction which alone can save forgiveness from becoming laxity; and this need is met by Christ's death. The Atonement is worked out according to the strict requirements of justice; God

receives compensation for man's default . . . . The relation of man
to God is treated by Anselm as essentially a legal relation, for his
whole effort is to prove that the atoning work is in accordance
with justice.[vii]

Likewise, writes Sloyin, "The one major flaw of [Anselm's] theory is that it
bases everything on the demand of divine justice, whereas Scripture presents
human salvation as a matter of the divine mercy or gratuity."[viii]
    Clearly, this "divine justice" that demands compensation, or "satisfaction,"
before the "the divine mercy" can provide salvation differs radically from
the justice of God revealed by the NT message.
    Paul's *good news about God's covenantal justice* (see Rom. 1:16-17), then,
stands in sharp contrast to Anselm's *bad news about God's legal justice*. In
fact, true to the Anselmian tradition, every contemporary presentation of the
evangelical "gospel" begins with the *bad news* that sinners stand condemned
as law-breakers in the sight of a "just" God, who demands that they pay
with the damnation of their souls. Only then can the so-called *good news* of
God's demand for payment having been *satisfied* by Jesus' death on the cross
be conveyed. For Anselm, and the evangelical doctrine of the atonement
that he formulated, *God's justice is the bad news*, which must be announced
before the good news of God's mercy can make sense.
    According to Brinsmead, the Protestant Reformer Martin

> Luther acknowledged that he could not understand Paul's gospel
> at first because he did not understand what the apostle meant
> when he said that the gospel revealed God's justice . . . . The
> Reformer's concept of God's justice was so influenced by Latin or
> Western thought that he could not understand why God's justice
> should cause him to sing and shout for joy. The Reformation
> was born when Luther began to understand the surprisingly
> kind face of God's justice. In the subsequent four hundred years
> Protestantism did little to develop Luther's pathfinding concept
> of God's justice.[ix]

    In historical fact, not only did it do "little to develop Luther's
pathfinding concept of God's justice," Protestant Christianity soon
rejected it out of hand out of allegiance to the legal concept of justice.
Despite challenging and rejecting many of the traditional doctrines
of Catholicism, the Protestant reformers (with the notable exceptions

of Luther and the so-called *radical reformers*, the Anabaptists), in an unbroken flow of tradition championed today by evangelical Christianity, embraced Anselm's theory of the atonement (as they did the Catholic doctrine of the Trinity, which is embedded in Anselm's theory). According to Aulen,

> The Latin doctrine of the Atonement is closely related to the legalism characteristic of the medieval outlook. Therefore, it ought to appear as a really amazing fact, that the post-Reformation theologians accepted the Anselmian doctrine of the Atonement without suspicion, altogether missing the close relation between this doctrine and the theological tradition which the Reformation had challenged with its watchword of *sola gratia* [Latin for "by grace alone"].[x]

At its root, the evangelical rhetoric of the cross is wholly inconsistent with the OT and the NT writers' concept of the justice of God. Unlike legal justice, which must exist in tension with mercy, God's covenantal justice is completely comfortable with freely forgiving sins and those who commit them. (And this is not to be confused with so-called "cheap grace" in that the covenantal justice of God empowers the recipients of God's faithfulness to reciprocate with a faithfulness of their own to God and neighbor.) Since the biblical God promises to forgive sins, his covenantal justice expresses itself in doing precisely that.

The biblical God did give a law (which is the subject of the next chapter), but its purpose was neither to reveal God's justice nor to justify God's people. While the element of payment in regard to the NT portrayal of Jesus' death on the cross is undeniable, it turns out to be equally undeniable that something other than the justice of God demanded it.

Endnotes

[i.] Robert Brinsmead, "The Scandal of God's Justice: Part 1," *The Christian Verdict*, 1983. <quango.net/brinsmead/scandalgodsjusticepart1.htm>.

[ii.] Gustav Aulen, *Christus Victor: An Historical Study of the Three Main Types of the Idea of Atonement* (New York: MacMillan, 1969), 81.

[iii.] Quoted from *De Poenitentia*, 6, by Aulen, 81.

[iv.] Aulen, 84.

v.   Ibid, 86.

vi.   Gerard S. Sloyin, *The Crucifixion of Jesus: History, Myth, Faith* (Minneapolis: Fortress Press, 1995),119.

vii.   Aulen, 89, 90.

viii.   Sloyin, 120.

ix.   Brinsmead.

x.   Aulen, 92.

CHAPTER 2

The Question of Law

At the heart of the evangelical rhetoric of the cross is the widely and deeply (and often unconsciously) held belief that the biblical God is, first and foremost, a God of law. While the biblical writers claim that God *gave* a law to one nation at one time and one place in history, the evangelical doctrine goes much further, resting squarely on the belief *that God's very nature is defined in terms of law.*

How this identification of God with law can be reconciled with Jesus' primary term of identification for God – "Father" – and with the clear NT claim that "God is love" (1 John 4:8) is a question that evangelical theologians have left largely unaddressed.

The biblical writers identify God with metaphors besides "Father," like "King" and "Judge," but these are not legal metaphors either. While the word of ancient kings may have been binding on their subjects, ancient kings were, for the most part, not law-makers but war-makers. Likewise, the Hebrew "judge" was not the presiding authority in a court of law, as in the Western tradition of jurisprudence; instead, judges, such as Gideon and Samson, were *leaders* of the people, especially in regard to delivering them from their oppressors.

In any case, the NT Jesus' preference for addressing God as "Father" – rather than as "King," even as he proclaimed "the kingdom of God" – placed love rather than law at the heart of the NT perception of God and his kingdom.

In fact, the NT Gospels portray not Jesus but his chief critics, the Pharisees, as the champions of law – albeit law in the form of "the tradition of the elders" (Matt. 15:2; Mark 7:5), which the Pharisaic tradition had formulated ostensibly to ensure careful observance of the Mosaic law. Indeed, a crucial flaw in the evangelical doctrine of the atonement is its assumption that the biblical God has the same view of law as had the Pharisees, as they were portrayed by the NT Gospels.

Just as the Pharisees believed that justification – that is, righteousness in God's sight – was earned by obeying the Mosaic law, so the evangelical rhetoric of the cross asserts that Jesus earned his righteousness in God's sight by rendering perfect obedience to the Mosaic law. As a result, God was able to justify – and, therefore, supposedly "forgive" – sinners on the basis of Jesus' perfect obedience along with the payment of his death for their sins.

The difference, then, between God and the Pharisees, as far as the evangelical doctrine is concerned, is not the belief that justification is the reward for obedience to the law; on this point the evangelical God agrees with the Pharisees. According to the evangelical theory, the difference between God and the Pharisees, rather, is that the Pharisees refused to acknowledge their guilt before God. That is, the Pharisees refused to acknowledge that they were not able to *perfectly* obey the Mosaic law.

Implicit in the evangelical rhetoric of the cross is the assumption that, had the Pharisees (or anyone else) been able to perfectly obey the Mosaic law, they *would* have been declared righteous by God, just as Jesus' righteousness is believed to have been due to his perfect obedience. But this is *the very essence of legalism*: the view that *righteousness can be earned by and, therefore, is the reward for performing works of law*.

It follows, then, that the evangelical God is the Arch Legalist, who orchestrated the crucifixion of Jesus, his Son, in order to uphold his law. The pained theological attempt to reconcile this thoroughly legalistic divine image with the NT image of God as loving Father has been assumed a glorious success by evangelical Christianity. But this schizophrenic "God" – torn between the legal obligation to condemn and the loving inclination to forgive – can hardly be persuasive to the human heart.

I

Understanding the biblical meaning of the word "law" and the role of the Mosaic law in the story of God's fulfillment of his Abrahamic promise is a prerequisite to understanding the NT meaning of the atonement.

The Hebrew word for "law" is *torah*, which is also the Jewish title for the first five OT books (i.e., *Torah*), known as "the books of the Law." The primary meaning of *torah* differs, however, from the primary English meaning of "law." The primary English sense of "law" is *legislation*, taking the form of an official code of conduct. By comparison, the Hebrew word *torah* means *instruction* or *guidance*. This Hebrew idea of law can include a legal code of conduct, which clearly provides guidance for behavior. Nevertheless, *torah* extends beyond legal codes to include stories and examples and other *wisdom-providing forms of guidance and instruction*.

If English readers of the Bible do not understand the broader, non-legislative use of the term "law" by the biblical writers, they will inevitably read into the biblical writers' portrayal of God the legalistic bent that is integral to the evangelical rhetoric of the cross.

The first five OT books were called *Torah* because they *instructed* Israel in its theological origins – that Israel *pre-existed* prophetically in God's promise to make of Abraham a great nation – and, thereby, the *Torah* provided *guidance* for Israel's future. By understanding its place in God's purpose for creation, Israel would be prepared to faithfully play its part. The stories of the creation and the flood along with the rise of the nations of the earth (see Genesis 1-11) form the background for Israel's origin in God's promise to Abraham to give him a son (see Gen. 15:1-6), through whom God would make of Abraham a great nation, through which God would eventually bless all nations (see Gen. 12:1-3 and 18:18). The biblical story of the patriarchs – Abraham, Isaac, and Jacob (the last of whom God renamed "Israel" and whose twelve sons became the twelve tribes of Israel) – forms the background for the emergence of the promised nation in the promised land. In its narrative function, *Torah* (i.e., the Law) tells the story of God's fulfillment of the promise to make of Abraham a great nation. As such, *Torah* included but was hardly limited to the ten commandments and the other regulations of the Mosaic law, the legal code of conduct which governed OT Israel.

The Mosaic law of commandments, then, was only part – and by no means the primary part – of *Torah*. Like the story of the Abrahamic promise, the initial fulfillment of which led to the national birth of Israel, the Mosaic law of commandments *also* provided instruction and guidance for Israel, albeit in the more direct form of imperatives (i.e., rules), rather than the narratives (i.e., stories) that led up to it, and which were considered *torah* (i.e., law) every bit as much as were the commandments. The story of the Abrahamic promise and its progressive fulfillment was the foundational element of the *Torah* in that the story of promise and fulfillment provided the *instruction* necessary – and, therefore, the indispensable context – for understanding the commandments.

Which is to say that the Mosaic law found its true meaning in the context of the Abrahamic promise that preceded it: the giving of the Mosaic law to govern Israel was instrumental in the fulfillment of God's promise to make of Abraham a great nation (and, therefore, to eventually bless all nations through Israel's Messiah).

The Abrahamic promise, therefore, was foundational to the Mosaic law, which served to administer the national fulfillment of the promise. In other words, the Mosaic law was given for the purpose of governing, during its residence in the promised land, the nation which God had promised to make of Abraham. God's covenant with Abraham – the promise of the son, the nation and the blessing to all nations – was obviously older than God's covenant with Israel (430 years older, according to Gal. 3:17).

Moreover, God's covenant with Israel was only the first part, or phase, of the fulfillment of God's previous covenant-promise to Abraham. As such, God's covenant with Israel administered the fulfillment of the *national* portion of the promise. The *national* portion of the promise was, in turn, the prerequisite to the subsequent fulfillment of the Abrahamic promise – the *international* portion of the promise – of blessing to all nations (see Gen. 12:1-3; 15:1-6; 18:18). This is why the NT writers called the Mosaic law the "old covenant": the Mosaic law was given to prepare Israel for the coming of its Messiah, through whom God would fulfill the final, and international, phase of the Abrahamic promise. While the "old covenant" (i.e., the Mosaic law) represented the *national fulfillment* of God's Abrahamic promise in the form of Israel, the "new covenant" represented the *international fulfillment* of the promise in the form of Israel's Messiah, in whom God would bless all nations.

Accordingly, Paul wrote, "the law, which came 430 years afterward [i.e., after God's promise to Abraham], does not annul a covenant previously ratified by God, so as to make the promise void" (Gal. 3:17). Paul addressed this point to those first-century Jews who were clinging to the old covenant (the Mosaic law), as if it were a permanent fixture in God's purpose, rather than embracing the new covenant. Rather than a permanent fixture, according to Paul, the Mosaic law was "added" to the Abrahamic promise "until the offspring [literally, 'the seed'] should come to whom the promise had been made" (Gal. 3:19). Paul identified "the seed" as "Christ" (Gal. 3:16), who had received the promise of imparting international blessing in the person of his ancestor Abraham (just as many centuries later, according to Heb. 7:9-10, Levi paid tithes to Melchizedek "through Abraham, for he was still in the loins of his ancestor when Melchizedek met him").

Paul's point was that, rather than being a *permanent fixture* in God's purpose for humanity – much less being integral to God's nature – the Mosaic law was a *temporary feature* of God's purpose. The Mosaic law, in other words, had a beginning and an end, *extending from the giving of the law to Moses to the dying on the cross of the Messiah*, the period of the "old covenant." During this period of time, the Mosaic law served a temporary purpose: to govern the nation of the Abrahamic promise, instructing and guiding Israel in the knowledge of the biblical God (in opposition to the false gods of the nations), in preparation for the coming of the Messiah, who would bring the final element of the promise – the blessing to all nations – to fulfillment. (Though other nations came under the influence of the Mosaic law through their interactions with Israel, no nation other than Israel received the Mosaic law – or any other law as far as the biblical writers were concerned – from God.)

In bringing to fulfillment God's Abrahamic promise to bless all nations, the Messiah would provide a new *torah*, or law, to instruct and guide God's people. But this new law would not be a legal code written in stone or on parchment, the legal code which Paul called "letter" (Rom. 7:6; 2 Cor. 3:6). Instead, the *torah* of the Messiah would be written, figuratively speaking, in human minds and on human hearts through the hearing and believing of the message of the righteousness – that is, the faithfulness-to-his-promise (see Chapter 1) – of God through his Messiah. Paul called this new *torah* "spirit," precisely because it would be written, through believing the new-covenant message, in the minds and on the hearts of God's people (Rom. 6:7; 2 Cor. 3:6). And to this righteousness, according to Paul, both "the Law and the Prophets bear witness" (Rom. 3:21), in the sense that both *Torah* and the OT prophets foretell the fulfillment of God's Abrahamic promise to bless all nations through his Messiah.

The historical moment God chose to banish the *old-covenant letter* in order to make way for the arrival of the *new-covenant spirit*, according to the NT writers, was the crucifixion of Jesus.

II

The old, or national, covenant between God and Israel consisted of the ten commandments of the Mosaic law: "And [Moses] wrote on the tablets the words of the covenant, the Ten Commandments" (Exo. 34:28). The other old-covenant commandments were applications of the ten commandments to specific cases, including prohibitions designed to insulate Israel from the surrounding nations' worship of "other gods" (Exo. 20:3), as well as ceremonial and sacrificial observances of "atonement," which were designed to express "a broken and contrite heart" (Psa. 51:17) for transgressions of the commandments, along with expressing reaffirmation of the covenant.

The NT Jesus viewed himself as the Messianic fulfillment of the Mosaic law along with the prophetic writings: "Do not think that I have come to abolish the Law or the Prophets; I have not come to abolish them but to fulfill them" (Matt. 5:17). Jesus, according to the NT writers, came to replace the old covenant with a new covenant, thereby replacing the rule of *the Mosaic law of commandments* with the rule of *the Messianic law of love*. But Jesus did not "come to abolish the Law," in the primary sense of *torah* as instruction and guidance. As Paul wrote, "But now the righteousness of God has been manifested apart from the law" – through the faith of God's Messiah, Jesus – "although the Law and the Prophets bear witness to it" (Rom. 3:21). Which is to say that, along with the prophetic books, the *Torah* – the first five books of the Bible – continues to "bear witness to" God's righteousness by telling its story of God's progressive fulfillment of his promise to make of Abraham a great nation through which he would eventually bless all nations.

Within the context of the overall story of the Mosaic law, defined as the first five OT books – from the creation of all things to the giving of the commandments through Moses – is the Mosaic law of commandments: the legal code that governed Israel beginning with its birth as a nation after its exodus from Egypt. As such it was a national covenant between God and Israel and came to an end with the inauguration of the new covenant between God and all nations (including, as the intended new-covenant leader of all nations, Israel).

Besides governing the nation, however, the Mosaic law also testified to God's Abrahamic promise. Every Israelite understood that the prologue to the ten commandments – "I am [*Yahweh*] your God, who brought you out of the land of Egypt, out of the house of slavery" (Exo. 20:2; Deut. 5:6) – meant that Israel's exodus from Egypt and nationhood in the promised land were the fulfillment of God's promise to make of Abraham a great nation.

Israel's obedience to the Mosaic law was intended, therefore, to express its faith in God's Abrahamic promise, that its election (i.e., its having-been-chosen) by God was due not to its own righteousness but to the righteousness (i.e., the covenant faithfulness) of its God: Israel's national identity was the fulfillment of God's promise. Therefore, Israel's righteousness would be a matter not of works of law per se but of faith in the promise, just as was Abraham's (Gen. 15:6; Deut. 6:25).

As it turned out, however, Israel did not manifest its faith in the promise through its obedience to the commandments. Instead, by being "disobedient" Israel manifested its "unbelief" (Heb. 3:18-19) regarding God's Abrahamic promise, and thus, its unrighteousness. The obedience required by the Mosaic law was not a perfect, in the *legal* sense of flawless, obedience; this would have equated righteousness with obedience to law in and of itself. Rather, the Mosaic law required *faithful* obedience: *perfect* in the *covenantal* sense of its representing a national rejection of other gods and a national commitment to the social (covenantal) justice of loving one's neighbor as oneself. The disobedience that brought Israel under judgment was its unfaithfulness to *Yahweh*, demonstrated by its following after the gods of the surrounding nations. Israel's idolatry inevitably resulted in social injustice, specifically in the form of the corruption of its worship into a religious system that validated the oppression and disenfranchisement of the poor by the rich (the social injustice that is endemic to any system of law, in which the rich will invariably find loopholes).

By bringing judgment on Israel for its national unfaithfulness (that is, its idolatry; see 2 Kgs. 17:7-23; Jer. 44:1-10), the Mosaic law gave to Israel "the knowledge of sin" (Rom. 3:20): Israel's "sin," of which the Mosaic law was intended to give it "knowledge," was not its transgressions of the Mosaic law per se; rather, Israel's "knowledge of sin" was intended to be both the collective and individual awareness of its unbelief regarding God's promise and, therefore, of its unfaithfulness to its God, a knowledge that was *manifested by* its transgressions of the Mosaic law, the first and foundational commandment being, "You shall have no other gods before me" (Exo. 20:3; Deut. 5:7).

To impart "the knowledge of sin" as unbelief regarding God's promise resulting in unfaithfulness to God, according to Paul, was the purpose for which God "added" the Mosaic law to the Abrahamic promise: "It was added because of transgressions . . ." (Gal. 3:19). The original language of the phrase "because of transgressions" can mean either that "transgressions" existed *before* the addition of the law or that "transgressions" existed *as the result of* the addition of the law. David J. Lull observes, "The current consensus is that this phrase expresses the result or goal of the Law: the Law 'was added for the sake of the transgressions,' which is to say, *to produce, generate,* or *provoke* them."[i] Likewise, according to F. F. Bruce, the phrase "expresses purpose, not antecedent cause. The law was brought into the situation as an additional factor, in order to produce transgressions."[ii]

This must, indeed, be the case because, as Paul wrote, "where there is no law there is no transgression" (Rom. 4:15). Which is *not* to say that sin does not exist in the absence of law: "for sin indeed was in the world before the law was given, but [as Paul clarifies] sin is not counted where there is no law" (Rom. 5:13).

Sin, in biblical terms, is defined *not* as transgression of God's law but as *unbelief manifested in the worship of other gods*, which is to say, *unfaithfulness to God*. Only when the worship of other gods was prohibited by the first commandment did "sin" become a matter of transgression. And, as a result, Israel's "sin" became a matter of public record, its unbelief being manifested in the form of its transgressions of the Mosaic law.

This biblical fact is devastating to the evangelical rhetoric of the cross, which insists that all human beings are accountable to some God-given "universal moral law" of God, of which the ten commandments are presumably a manifestation. The evangelical doctrine depends on this notion because it underlies God's obligation to demand payment for the transgressions of all of his human creatures.

Human accountability to God does not, however, require that all human beings find themselves under a God-given law.

For the biblical writers, all of God's human creatures are accountable to God by virtue of the act of creation, which makes God known to all, if only implicitly, as Creator. To have been "created . . . in the image of God" (Gen. 1:27) is to be accountable to reflect that image. God's covenantal relationship with humanity is clearly indicated – even in the absence of the term "covenant" – in the creation story, according to which God entrusts humanity with the stewardship of the rest of creation (see Gen. 1:26-31). Humanity is God's agent, responsible to exercise benevolent "dominion over" – which is to say, stewardship, as opposed to the exploitation and desecration, of – creation on God's behalf. Following the Creator's first judgment of the world by water, God makes with "Noah and his sons" an explicit "covenant" that extends not only to their "offspring" but also to "every living creature that is with you," promising that "never again shall there be a flood to destroy the earth" (Gen. 9:8-11). This can only be a renewal of the original covenant of God with humanity (as indicated by Gen. 9:6-7). The fact that it is made with "every living creature" indicates that this universal covenant exists, for the biblical writers, even with human beings who are ignorant of it.

This universal covenant was confirmed by Paul, for whom humans are accountable to God not because of any universal moral law but because "what can be known about God is plain to them, [being] clearly perceived, ever since the creation of the world, in the things that have been made" (Rom. 1:19, 20). For Paul, humanity is accountable for having "exchanged the truth about God for a lie and worshiped and served the creature rather than the Creator" (Rom. 1:25), which is to identify "sin" as universal covenantal unfaithfulness. Consequently, "all who sinned without the law will also perish without the law" (Rom. 2:11), no God-given law being necessary to justify God's judgment.[1] Paul's universal indictment of humanity that "all have sinned and fall short of the glory of God" (Rom. 3:23) does not necessitate a law that "all" have transgressed. In keeping with the literal meaning of the word rendered "sin" (Greek, *hamartia*: to miss the mark), the biblical *mark* that "all" have missed is not a God-given legal standard of righteousness but *God himself*, insofar as all have, in one form or another, "exchanged the truth about God for a lie and worshiped and served the creature rather than the Creator."[2]

No law, then, was necessary, as far as the NT writers were concerned, to hold humanity accountable to its Creator, whose justice is not *legal* but *covenantal*, providing justification and salvation for all who seek his face and heed his call. And if human accountability to God is *covenantal* rather than *legal*, then the entire legal foundation of the evangelical doctrine of the atonement crumbles. The notion that all human beings are transgressors of a God-given law, which requires God, if he is to be just, to demand payment for transgressions, turns out to be without biblical foundation.

Besides this creation-based accountability it shared with all nations, the biblical writers hold Israel to a greater, because a more clearly informed, accountability to God. The commandments of the Mosaic law specified and itemized Israel's accountability in terms of "transgressions." By prohibiting

---

[1] Paul's reference to "Gentiles, who do not have the law, [doing] what the law requires [and, therefore, showing] that the work of the law is written on their hearts" (Rom. 2:14, 15) concerns not unbelieving Gentiles but Gentile believers, who are Jews "inwardly [because] circumcision is a matter of the heart, by the Spirit, not by the letter" (Rom. 2:29).

[2] Thus, according to the NT writers, the necessity for faith in the biblical message to be counted righteous: apart from hearing the message about God's revelation of his purpose through his promise to Abraham and its fulfillment in the Messiah, human beings remain ignorant of the biblical God and, therefore, enslaved to the worship of "the creature rather than the Creator."

the worship of "other gods" (Exo. 20:3) and the social injustices that resulted from such worship, the Mosaic law produced "transgressions" – that is, specific violations of written law – thereby becoming a record, along with the prophetic testimony, of Israel's sin, that is, its unbelief regarding God's Abrahamic promise and subsequent unfaithfulness to God. The purpose of this Mosaic-prophetic record of the sin of Israel, then, was to impart to the Israelites (at least to those with ears to hear) a "knowledge of sin" (Rom. 3:20).

When "sin came into the world" through Adam (Rom. 5:12), an explosion of natural consequences – consequences not only for human nature but also, according to Paul, for the natural world (see Rom. 8:19-22) – was ignited. Though the first sin consisted of the breaking of a commandment, the biblical definition of sin is not the breaking of law,[3] God's having given only one law to one nation for one period of time. Instead, sin is the breaking of faith with God, which is what the so-called "original sin" of Adam means. Once this rupture occurred, perpetuated by human "hardness of heart" and its compulsion toward self-justification, the repairing of the relationship (i.e., the righteousness) of faith between God and humanity could only be worked out in the context of the biblical story of promise and fulfillment.

All of which is to say that the biblical writers define sin not in *legal* terms but in *covenantal*, or relational, terms. Just as biblical righteousness is not law-keeping but faith-keeping, so biblical sin is not law-breaking but faith-breaking (see Chapter 1).

If the definition of sin were transgression of God's law, then non-Israelites could not sin because Israel was the only nation to receive a law from God. To the contrary, however, the biblical definition of sin encompasses both Israel and the nations, all of which rejected the *God of promise* in favor of "other gods." According to the biblical writers, Israel was the more culpable to the extent that the nations worshipped their gods out of relative ignorance of the biblical God whereas Israel repeatedly forsook the God it ostensibly

---

[3]   That "sin is lawlessness" (1 John 3:4) does not mean that sin is the breaking of a law. The term "lawlessness" must be understood in terms of the Hebrew word for law (*torah*), which means instruction and guidance. That "sin is lawlessness" means that sin is the rejection of God's instruction and guidance, whether revealed through creation, the Mosaic law, or the NT message. Biblically speaking, sin is a breaking of faith with God and, therefore, a rejection of God's *torah*, that is, guidance.

knew to follow after the gods of the nations. The problem was that the Mosaic law could not provide a deep and abiding knowledge of God that would produce faithfulness.

III

Nevertheless, the Mosaic law had its part to play between the Abrahamic promise and its Messianic fulfillment: "For by works of the law no human being will be justified in his sight, since through the law comes knowledge of sin" (Rom. 3:20). And in the performance of its educational role in the history of old-covenant Israel, the Mosaic law became a record of the sins of the people, *constituting a legal debt that demanded payment.*

This individual and collective sense of legal debt, created by individual and national transgressions of the Mosaic law, explains the educational role of the animal sacrifices in the Mosaic legal system. The evangelical idea that the animal sacrifices exhibit God's old-covenant demand for payment misunderstands their function.

The animal sacrifices were required by the law as an acknowledgement on the part of Israel of its unfaithfulness to *Yahweh* and an expression of the people's individual and collective will to be faithful (see Psa. 51:16-19). As such, the animal sacrifices were able to provide only a ceremonial sense of the restoration of fellowship with *Yahweh* that had been broken by Israel's unfaithfulness:

> For since the law has but a shadow of the good things to come instead of the true form of these realities, it can never, by the same sacrifices that are continually offered every year, make perfect those who draw near. Otherwise, would they not have ceased to be offered, since the worshipers, having once been cleansed, would no longer have any consciousness of sin? (Heb. 10:1-2)

The notion that the biblical God required blood in order to forgive confuses the biblical God with the law *Yahweh* temporarily gave to Israel to convey "knowledge of sin" (Rom. 3:20). It was *not God but the Mosaic law* that required blood before forgiveness was a possibility: "Indeed, under the law almost everything is purified with blood, and without the shedding of blood there is no forgiveness of sins" (Heb. 9:22). To point out that purification "with blood" is required "under the law" is to make that requirement a function of the law itself. And if true that the Mosaic law was a temporary feature of, rather than a permanent fixture in, God's purpose, then the requirement of "blood" for "forgiveness" is not a requirement inherent in any sense in the nature of the biblical God.

Moreover, the Hebrew writer's point is not that the Mosaic law *could* provide forgiveness with "the shedding of blood." The function of a legal system is, after all, to prohibit and punish transgressions, not to forgive them. Rather, for the Israelites to experience a sense of *Yahweh*'s forgiveness, that is, the ongoing renewal, despite their unfaithfulness, of their sense of *having-been-chosen-by-God*, even in a ceremonial – that is, a temporary and superficial – way, the demand of the Mosaic law for the punishment of transgressors had to be neutralized, in the sense of pacified, or appeased. This was the effect of the animal sacrifices.

The purpose of the sacrifices commanded by the Mosaic law, then, was not to satisfy *Yahweh*'s demand for payment – as was the purpose of pagan sacrifices to their gods, thereby purchasing the favor of the gods. Instead, the purpose of the Mosaic sacrifices was, on one hand, to require the Israelites to take into account their unfaithfulness to *Yahweh* and, on the other, to provide them with a limited, ceremonial sense of their ongoing election by *Yahweh* – their continued *chosen-ness* – and of *Yahweh*'s unceasing love for them.

Nevertheless, "in these sacrifices there is a reminder of sin every year. For it is impossible for the blood of bulls and goats to take away sins" (Heb. 10:3-4). Which is to say that a deep and abiding and transforming sense of God's love in human hearts would require a *new covenant*, inaugurated by a sacrifice of another kind.

Therefore, according to the primary sense of *torah* as instruction/guidance, the educational purpose of the Mosaic law – to provide Israel with "the knowledge of sin" (Rom. 3:20) as *unbelief-and-unfaithfulness toward the God of promise* – was facilitated by the animal sacrifices insofar as they imparted to the Israelites a sense of ongoing fellowship, however limited, with their God. By comparison, according to the NT writers, the sacrifice of God's Messiah for the sins of God's people would free them fully and forever from the condemnation of the Mosaic law for a deep and abiding assurance of God's forgiveness, that is, of God's ongoing and unceasing acceptance.

Through its testimony, first, about Abraham's faith in God's promise to make of him a great nation and to bless all nations through his seed and, second, about sin as the unbelief of Israel regarding God's Abrahamic promise, the Mosaic law served to guide a faithful "remnant" of Israel (Rom.

11:5) to faith in its coming Messiah. And the Messiah of Israel, according to the OT prophets, would fulfill God's Abrahamic promise to bless all nations, incorporating them into the new-covenant freedom of his people from the condemnation of the Mosaic law.

Jesus, while coming to bring an end to the legislative rule of the commandments of the Mosaic law over God's people, did not come to abolish the Mosaic law in its instructional capacity as *torah*. Instead, he came to fulfill it by bringing to pass its testimony about the Messianic fulfillment of God's promise to bless all nations in Abraham's seed: "And beginning with Moses and all the Prophets, he interpreted to them in the Scriptures the things concerning himself" (Luke 24:27).

This is also Paul's explanation of the continuing role of the Mosaic law, along with the OT prophetic literature: "But now the righteousness of God has been manifested apart from the law [that is, through the NT message], although the Law and the Prophets bear witness to it . . ." (Rom. 3:21). Consequently, while the Mosaic law continues to serve as *torah*, by *instructing* and *guiding* God's people in its "witness" to God's righteousness as a righteousness of faith, and to sin as unbelief-and-unfaithfulness toward God, the Mosaic law as the legal code that governed God's people under the old covenant came to an end with the arrival of Israel's Messiah and, more specifically, at his death on the cross.

While the Pharisees viewed the Mosaic law as an end in itself which would remain forever as the mediator between God and his people (who would forever, as far the Pharisees were concerned, be confined to the nation of Israel), Jesus viewed the Mosaic law as the means to an end: "You search the Scriptures [i.e., 'Moses and all the Prophets'] because you think that in them you have eternal life; and it is they that bear witness about me, yet you refuse to come to me that you may have life" (John 5:39-40).

For Paul, as for the NT Jesus himself, the coming, and specifically the sacrifice, of the Messiah necessarily meant the end of the Mosaic law – the perfection, or completion, of the old covenant in the form of a new covenant – in terms of its role as mediator between God and his people: "For Christ is the end of the law for righteousness to everyone who believes" (Rom. 10:4). According to Paul, Israel's Messiah is "the end" (Greek, *telos*) of the Mosaic law in the sense of being its fulfillment, its purpose, its reason for being in the first place.

Once again, God "added" the Mosaic law to the Abrahamic promise (430 years after the promise was made, according to Gal. 3:17) only "until the [seed] should come to whom the promise had been made" (Gal. 3:19).

The Messianic "seed" of Abraham having come, the temporary role of the Mosaic law in the government of God's people necessarily came to an end. The time of the *national* covenant – between God and Israel – concluded with the establishing of the *international* covenant, according to which "Gentiles" (Greek, *ethne*, from *ethnos*: nations) would be "grafted in" to Israel (Rom. 11:13, 17, 23-24).

Through faith in the NT message, Israel would literally take its place as the first among "all nations" to receive the promised international blessing of God, just as "all nations" would, through faith in the same message, be figuratively "grafted in" to "the Israel of God" (Gal. 6:16). This could only happen with the termination of the national and legal covenant between God and Israel, Israel subsequently becoming the new-covenant home of all nations through the sacrifice of God's Messiah Jesus.

IV

If the Mosaic law was given by God to a single nation (i.e., Israel) for a single duration (i.e., from Moses to Messiah), and if the NT meaning of Jesus' death on the cross is the termination of the Mosaic law, how can the NT writers say that Jesus died for the sins of all? How is it that Gentiles, who did not receive the Mosaic law from God, also receive the benefit of Jesus' death, if the purpose of his death was to bring an end of the Mosaic law?

The biblical (and Hebrew) concept of *collective identity* is central to an understanding of the Hebrew God's dealings both with his people in particular and with humanity in general. The biblical word of God is addressed to God's people, who are God's people because they hear and believe God's word. At the same time, the biblical word of God is addressed to all people in that anyone who hears God's word is, thereby, called to believe and, therefore, to become one of God's people. Biblically speaking, then, all people are *potentially* God's people in the hearing of God's word and *actually* God's people in the believing of the word. God's people are, thus, a *collective identity – all who hear and believe the word of God –* with which individuals are free to identify themselves, through believing when they hear the word of God, or to choose not to identify themselves through unbelief.

Moreover, God's people as a *collective identity* in God's mind have been the object of God's purpose from the beginning, before any specific historical individuals chose either to believe God's word, and therefore, identify themselves with God's people, or to reject God's word and remain outside of that *collective identity*.

For the NT writers, "Israel" began as a *collective national identity*, the nation of physical descendants of Abraham, and – following the proclamation-crucifixion-resurrection-and-exaltation of God's Messiah – became a *collective spiritual identity* consisting of believing residents of all nations, beginning with the remnant of Israel. The *collective identity* of God's people was *spiritually/rhetorically*[4] transformed from a single nation to an international community at the inauguration of the new covenant. This development corresponded to the progressive fulfillment of God's promise to give Abraham a son (Isaac), through whom God would make of Abraham a great nation (Israel), through which God would bless all nations (in Israel's Messiah).

That Israel's Messiah would be the instrument through whom God would bless all nations necessarily meant that the Messiah would also be the instrument through whom God would end his exclusive national relationship with Israel.

When Israel's Messiah died and rose from the dead to fulfill the Abrahamic promise of blessing for all nations, the *collective identity* of God's people was expanded from those old-covenant Israelites who had believed the word of God to include new-covenant believers of all nations. And "Israel" – in the form of the Jewish followers of Jesus – became no longer the single nation of God's people but the leading nation in, and the nation that would expand to include, the international community of faith. Which is to say that Israel at last became the "light for the nations" (Isa. 49:6) that *Yahweh*, through the OT prophets, had both called Israel to be and promised that Israel would one day become.

Accordingly, the NT writers assert that the atonement applies, at the same time, to God's people *and* to all people. Jesus died for God's people, to redeem them from bondage to the Mosaic law, and anyone, Jew or Gentile, who hears and believes the NT message thereby enters not the old covenant

---

[4]   What is *spiritual*, biblically speaking, is what is *revealed* regarding God's purpose from the beginning, to be realized eschatologically at the coming of the kingdom of God. Therefore, what is *spiritual* is also *rhetorical* in that what is *spiritual* is *revealed in the NT words of Jesus and his apostles* for the express purpose of *persuading hearers* to believe the NT gospel. See John 6:63 and 1 Cor. 2:10-13 for the identification of "spirit" and "spiritual" with the revelation, that is the "words," of Jesus and the apostles.

of condemnation but the new covenant of forgiveness. That is, the covenant of *the life-giving spirit* of the Messianic faith rather than *the killing letter* of the Mosaic law (see 2 Cor. 3:6).

The major conflict within the first-century community of Jesus-followers, according to the NT writers, was whether or not Gentile believers in the NT message must observe the Mosaic law. The consensus among first-century practitioners of Pharisaic Judaism was that the Mosaic law was everlasting. Contrary to the belief that the Messiah would come to bring an end to the Mosaic law, the most popular Messianic expectation in first-century Judea seems to have been that God would fulfill his Abrahamic promise to bless all nations by sending the Messiah to lead a military insurrection that would, first, overthrow the Roman empire and, subsequently, bring all nations under the rule of the Mosaic law, administered by the newly restored and now imperial nation of Israel: *this would be the kingdom of God.*

This was, in fact, the crux of the argument between Paul and not only the Judean religious establishment, which rejected the Messiahship of Jesus, but also the many so-called "Judaizers," those Jewish believers who insisted that Gentile believers be required to observe the Mosaic law: Was the Mosaic law, as Paul argued, a temporary and structural feature of God's purpose or was it, according to the majority Jewish view, a permanent and foundational fixture in God's purpose?

Francis Watson uses the intertestamental literature,[5] which reveals so much regarding the theological assumptions of the second-temple Judaism of Jesus' and Paul's day, to show that the predominant first-century Jewish belief was that the Mosaic law was foundational to God's relationship with Israel. Which is to say that, contrary to Paul's insistence that God's Abrahamic promise was the historical and theological foundation on which the Mosaic law was built – the promise having been made 430 years prior to the law's being given – the Jewish assumption was that the law took priority over the promise, somehow even existing prior to it:

> In those [intertestamental] texts, Abraham, Isaac and Jacob do
> not inhabit a kind of law-free zone, living by promise alone. Their

---

[5]   The intertestamental literature encompasses noncanonical Jewish writings from approximately 600 to 5 B.C., including the apocrypha and the pseudepigrapha.

relationship with God is already determined in advance by the Torah, to which they show an exemplary obedience. There is, then, no divine covenant with Israel which can be differentiated from the covenant enacted at Mount Sinai. Unlike Paul, the texts in question all presuppose that the Sinai covenant is the enduring foundation of the divine-human relationship; it is therefore inconceivable to them that God's gracious election of Israel should have been established somewhere other than at Sinai. That means, however, that the question of Israel's observance or non-observance of the law is fundamental to the covenant itself.[iii]

The intertestamental literature, then, appears to invert the historical covenantal order, thereby making the giving of the Mosaic law at Sinai foundational to the making of the Abrahamic promise, which thereby becomes subordinate to and dependent on the Mosaic law:

> What is at issue is whether the covenant with Abraham constitutes the *basis* of God's covenant with Israel, to which the Sinai event is simply a very important *addition*. And the answer is clear: the Sinai event itself is basic, and the covenant with Abraham is subsumed within it. Ben Sira has this to say about Abraham:

> Abraham was the great father of a multitude of nations, and no-one has been found like him in glory. He kept the law of the Most High, and was taken into covenant with him; he established the covenant in his flesh, and when he was tested he was found faithful. Therefore the Lord assured him by an oath that the nations would be blessed through his posterity . . . (Sir.44.19-21)

> Here too, law and covenant are virtual synonyms. Abraham was indeed the privileged recipient of divine promises, but he received these promises as one who 'kept the law of the Most High' – an apparently general reference to a life of obedience to a law that had not yet been fully disclosed, although it is followed by a more specific reference to circumcision, 'the covenant in his flesh'. The promises are brought within the scope of the covenant given through Moses at Sinai, when (to quote from the following chapter)

> [God] made him hear his voice, and led him into the thick darkness, and gave him the commandments face to face, the law of life and knowledge, to teach Jacob the covenant, and Israel his judgments. (45.5)

> As already in Deuteronomy, the promises to the patriarchs are inseparable from 'the law of life and knowledge', God's covenant with Israel. *Observance of the law is basic to Israel's existence as the covenant people of God.* It is not the case that observance of the law occurs on the basis of a divine election that is already established prior to the law.[iv]

The testimony of Ben Sira and other intertestamental texts is significant because it reveals the bedrock first-century Jewish assumptions that made Paul's proclamation of a Mosaic-law-free covenant between God and Israel – an "Israel" that included believers of all nations – virtually unthinkable to the Jewish mind (which is why not only Gentiles but also Jews had to experience *repentance* [Greek, *metanoia*, literally, *change of mind*] in order to believe the NT message.)

Paul's historical argument that because the Abrahamic promise preceded the Mosaic law by 430 years, the promise must take precedence over the law, which must itself be temporary rather than permanent, constituted a radical paradigm shift for the Jews of his day. For first-century Jews, this ideological paradigm shift was religious but not only religious in the limited contemporary sense, for their religion was not only identical to their culture but also to their national identity. First-century Judaism represented as fierce a nationalism as any in the history of nations. And the focus of Jewish nationalism was the Mosaic law.

That Jesus' proclamation of the kingdom of God constituted a rejection not only of imperial Rome but also of the imperial ambitions of Jewish nationalism meant, in the first place, that Jesus' execution was inevitable, and in the second, that Paul's proclamation of Jesus' gospel would make him a flashpoint of controversy not only among his fellow Jews but also in the first-century community of both Jewish and Gentile followers of Jesus.

The intimate relationship between first-century Jewish nationalism and the Mosaic law seems rarely to have been connected by Christian theologians to the meaning of the atonement. Paul certainly made the connection:

Therefore remember that at one time you Gentiles in the flesh, called "the uncircumcision" by what is called the circumcision, which is made in the flesh by hands – remember that you were at that time separated from Christ, alienated from the commonwealth of Israel and strangers to the covenants of promise, having no hope and without God in the world. But now in Christ Jesus you who once were far off have been brought near by the blood of Christ. For he himself is our peace, who has made us both one and has broken down in his flesh the dividing wall of hostility by abolishing the law of commandments and ordinances, that he might create in himself one new man in place of the two, so making peace, and might reconcile us both to God in one body through the cross, thereby killing the hostility. And he came and preached peace to you who were far off and peace to those who were near. For through him we both have access in one Spirit to the Father. (Eph. 2:11-18)

The Mosaic law was "the dividing wall of hostility" between Jew and Gentile in that the Jewish religious establishment used the Mosaic law not only to justify (and, therefore, from the NT Jesus' standpoint, to condemn) itself through its observance of "the tradition of the elders" (Matt. 15:2; Mark 7:3) but also to condemn and, thereby to exclude, the nations for their idolatry. (God had, according to a popular saying, created Gentiles to "fuel the fires of Gehenna.")

The Mosaic law was essential to the preservation of the first-century Jewish national identity as the people of God, as distinct from and opposed to the idolatrous nations of the world. As such, the law constituted an insurmountable barrier to the emergence of an international community of faith in the biblical God, and therefore, an insurmountable barrier to the fulfillment of God's Abrahamic promise to bless all nations. As long as the rule of the Mosaic law over God's people stood, therefore, the law would condemn not only Israel, due to its transgressions, but all nations as well, by portraying Israel's God as their adversary and, therefore, deepening their alienation from God's purpose and further excluding them from the knowledge of the biblical God.

The *letter* of the Mosaic law had to be replaced by the *spirit* of the Messianic law in order for Gentiles, first, to realize that the God of Israel was the God of all nations and, second, to rise to equal standing with Jews among the people of God. Reconciliation to God for both Jew and Gentile, in the form of a Mosaic-law-free covenantal relationship between God and his people, as far as Paul was concerned, necessitated the termination of the rule of the Mosaic law.

Once first-century Gentiles heard and believed the NT message, they became part of the collective "we" and "us" of God's people. So, when Paul wrote to the Gentile believers of Galatia that "Christ redeemed *us* from the curse of the law by becoming a curse for *us*" (Gal. 3:13), he addressed these Gentile believers as if they had been included with Jews under the condemnation of the Mosaic law. As Gentiles, however, they had not been under the Mosaic law at all, being (like all Gentiles) "strangers to the covenants of promise" (Eph. 2:12). Nevertheless, now that these Gentiles had believed the NT message and, therefore, become God's people, they had identified themselves with God's people as a *collective identity*. That is, they were now among the "us" whom "Christ redeemed . . . from the curse of the law."

Unless faith in the NT message meant, for Gentiles, freedom from the obligation to obey the Mosaic law, then faith in the NT message would have been self-contradictory, offering salvation but issuing condemnation. If Gentile believers had been required to obey the Mosaic law as a condition of identification with God's people – as Gentile converts to Judaism had always been required to do – they would have, as surely as had the Jews, stood condemned by the law. (This was, of course, the issue that Paul addressed and intended to resolve in his letter to the Galatians.)

In NT terms, unbelieving Gentiles do not perish because of their sins – as if God were unwilling to forgive them. Instead, unbelieving Gentiles perish, just like unbelieving Jews, because of unbelief. As Paul explained, "for sin indeed was in the world before the law was given, but sin is not counted where there is no law" (Rom. 5:13). Law is for the purpose of counting sin in the form of transgressions in order to give "knowledge of sin" (Rom. 3:20). Sin itself is not breaking God's law but breaking faith with God, just as righteousness is a matter not of law-keeping but of faith-keeping. Breaking faith with God doesn't require breaking a law from God; it simply means worshiping "the creature rather than the Creator" (Rom. 1:25).

In sum, the biblical judgment, according to the NT writers, is that all perish due to unbelief, and all – both Jews and Gentiles – experience forgiveness of sins as a Mosaic-law-free covenantal relationship with God through faith in the NT message.

V

Whereas obedience to the Mosaic law was the means whereby God's old-covenant people expressed their faith in the Abrahamic promise, the new covenant replaced obedience to the Mosaic law with obedience to the Messianic law as the way faith in the Abrahamic promise would be expressed by God's new-covenant people. And to obey the Messianic law would not be to "serve in oldness of letter," that is, to observe a code of conduct. Instead, to obey the Messianic law would be to "serve in newness of spirit," that is, to believe the new-covenant message of God's love for one and all in his Messiah and to love oneself and one's neighbor accordingly (quotations are literal renderings of Rom. 7:6).

The role of the Mosaic law in the government of God's people, then, was replaced by the Messianic law, according to the NT writers. Consequently, to believe the Messianic gospel and to behave accordingly is to obey the Messianic *torah* – "the law of Christ" (Gal. 6:2): The NT message is now the *torah* of God's people, providing the *instruction and guidance* for a life of "faith working through love" (Gal. 5:6).

Jesus implied the end of the governing role of the Mosaic law by identifying "the great commandment in the Law" as follows: "You shall love the Lord your God with all your heart and with all your soul and with all your mind . . . . And a second is like it: You shall love your neighbor as yourself." Jesus made clear that his intention was to sum up the Mosaic law by adding, "On these two commandments depend all the Law and the Prophets" (Matt. 22:36, 37, 39-40). Which is to say that love for God (to the exclusion of other, religious or secular, gods) and love for neighbor were God's will for his people from the beginning. Assuming faith in the God of the Abrahamic promise, the Golden Rule sums up all the commandments: "So whatever you wish that others would do to you, do also to them, for this is the Law and the Prophets" (Matt. 7:12).

Likewise, for Paul,

> . . . the one who loves another has fulfilled the law. The commandments, "You shall not commit adultery, You shall not murder, You shall not steal, You shall not covet," and any other commandment, are summed up in this word: "You shall love your neighbor as yourself." Love does no wrong to a neighbor: therefore, love is the fulfilling of the law. (Rom. 13:8-10)

And so, Paul's summary of the *Messianic law*: "Bear one another's burdens, and so fulfill the law of Christ" (Gal. 6:2). The one who hears the NT message is called, first, to believe the message and, second, to love oneself and, therefore, others as the message reveals that God loves one and all. Likewise, "And this is his commandment, that we believe in the name of his Son Jesus Christ and love one another, just as he has commanded us" (1 John 3:23).

This replacement of the Mosaic law of commandments by the Messianic law of love is the replacement of the old covenant by the "new covenant" prophesied by Jeremiah (and echoed in Heb. 8:8-12):

> Behold, the days are coming, declares [*Yahweh*], when I will make a new covenant with the house of Israel and the house of Judah, not like the covenant that I made with their fathers on the day when I took them by the hand to bring them out of the land of Egypt, my covenant that they broke, though I was their husband, declares [*Yahweh*]. But this is the covenant that I will make with the house of Israel after those days, declares [*Yahweh*]: I will put my law within them, and I will write it on their hearts. I will be their God, and they shall be my people. And no longer shall each one teach his neighbor and each his brother, saying, "Know [*Yahweh*]," for they shall all know me, from the least of them to the greatest, declares [*Yahweh*]. For I will forgive their iniquity, and I will remember their sin no more. (Jer. 31:31-34)

With the coming of Israel's Messiah, *Yahweh* promised to "put my law within them" and to "write it on their hearts." And how would *Yahweh* do this? By replacing the Mosaic law, which Paul called the old-covenant "letter," with the Messianic gospel, which Paul called the new-covenant "spirit" (Rom. 7:6; 2 Cor. 3:6).

In the cases of both *torah-as-letter* and *torah-as-spirit*, *torah* is a matter of words. In the latter case, however, the words are "written not with ink but with the Spirit of the living God, not on tablets of stone but on tablets of human hearts" (2 Cor. 3:3).

The inner working of "the Spirit of the living God" is the work of the NT message itself, writing God's *torah* on believing hearts by means of persuasion, as opposed to the coercion of *torah-as-letter*. God's old-covenant *torah-as-letter* was coercive in that, like any written code of law, it functioned by threatening immediate, or at least imminent, punishment for transgressions. By comparison, God's new-covenant *torah-as-spirit* is persuasive in that, while warning believers to prepare for the inevitable end of the present age, it motivates by instilling in believing hearts the knowledge of God's love.

For Paul, believing the NT message meant, figuratively speaking, that "God's love has been poured into our hearts through the Holy Spirit . . ." (Rom. 5:5). Believers learn – via the *instruction and guidance* of the Messianic *torah* – to love one another and others just as the NT message reveals that God has loved one and all in his Messiah.

The coercive power of *torah-as-letter* was necessary during the time prior to the the coming of the Messiah. Under the old covenant, *Yahweh's* people "were held captive under the law, imprisoned until the coming faith would be revealed. So then, the law was our guardian until Christ came, in order that we might be justified by faith" (Gal. 3:23-24). Which is to say that under the Mosiac law, God's people were in their childhood:

> I mean that the heir, as long as he is a child, is no different from a slave, though he is the owner of everything, but he is under guardians and managers until the date set by his father. In the same way we also, when we were children, were enslaved to the elementary principles of the world. (Gal. 4:1-3)

Just as legal justice can be understood as a necessary evil, in the relative absence of God's covenantal justice in the world (see Chapter 1), so the Mosaic law was a kind of necessary evil, enslaving God's people "to the elementary principles of the world," until they were ready to enter the maturity of faith, which corresponded to the fulfillment of God's promise to bless all nations in the seed of Abraham.

With the crucifixion-and-resurrection of the Messiah, however, the coercion of law (*torah-as-letter*) had been replaced by the persuasion of faith (*torah-as-spirit*): "But now that faith has come, we are no longer under a guardian, for in Christ Jesus you are all sons of God, through faith" (Gal. 3:25-26). Which is not to say that "faith" did not exist under the old covenant – as it certainly did among the OT faithful (see Hebrews 11). Nevertheless, under *torah-as-letter*, faith could not become widespread within Israel, and therefore could never spread from Israel to all nations, because faith could never, under *torah-as-letter*, reach maturity. Only with the coming of the faith of Israel's Messiah could Israel – in the form of Jesus' apostles and the first-century apostolic community – become "a light for the nations" (Isa. 49:6), so that God could fulfill his promise to bless all nations.

Israel could not realize the maturity of faith under *torah-as-letter* – a legal system of coercion – just as children cannot realize maturity as long as they live under parental rules and regulations. The loving coercion of parental rules and regulations is a temporary expedient designed to gradually prepare children for the maturity of adulthood, which can only be experienced once children are old enough to be freed from parental authority. Likewise, the Mosaic law was God's temporary and loving expedient for gradually preparing his people for the spiritual adulthood of sonship in their Messiah, according to whose faith their lives would be governed not by the coercion of *torah-as-letter* but by the persuasion of *torah-as-spirit*:

> But when the fullness of time had come, God sent forth his Son, born of woman, born under the law, to redeem those who were under the law, so that we might receive adoption as sons. And because you are sons, God has sent the Spirit of his Son into our hearts, crying, "Abba! Father!" So you are no longer a slave, but a son, and if a son, then an heir through God. (Gal. 4:4-7)

Accordingly, with the coming of Israel's Messiah and his *torah-as-spirit*, the time of the Mosaic law's rule over God's people – the time of *torah-as-letter* – came to an end. The old covenant had fulfilled its role in God's purpose: "In speaking of a new covenant, [God] makes the first one obsolete" (Heb. 8:13).

The biblical God, then, turns out not to be a God of law after all. Just as this God's justice is not *legal* but *covenantal*, so God is not a God of *law* but a God of *promise*. And just as no tension exists between God's justice and mercy – the covenantal justice of God freely providing forgiveness of sins to believers – so no tortured logic is necessary to the understanding that the biblical God of promise *is* love.

The God of promise expressed his love for all nations by bringing his old *national* covenant with Israel to an end in order to bless all nations, beginning with Israel – as Paul wrote, "to the Jew first and also to the Greek" (Rom. 1:16) – in the context of a new *international* covenant. And the depth and breadth of God's love is measured by the NT claim that the termination of the rule of the old-covenant law (its termination synonymous, as shall be shown, with the forgiveness of sins) required the death of his Son, Israel's Messiah, on a Roman cross.

Endnotes

i.   David J. Lull, "The Law as Our Pedagogue: A Study in Galatians 3:19-25." *Journal of Biblical Literature:* vol. 105. no. 3. (Sept. 1986): 483.

ii. F. F. Bruce, *New International Greek Testament Commentary: Commentary on Galatians* (Grand Rapids: Eerdman's, 1982), 175.

iii. Francis Watson, "Not the New Perspective." An unpublished paper delivered at the British New Testament Conference. Manchester, September 2001, 10.

iv. Ibid. 11-12.

CHAPTER 3

The Question of Wrath

The NT claim that "God is love" (1 John 4:8) must somehow be reconciled with the biblical indications that the OT God of Israel, whose name was *Yahweh*, seems to have had a dark side. The genocidal tendencies of the Israelites, in their *Yahweh*-ordained conquest of and residence in the promised land, is not easy to reconcile with the biblical God's love for all nations. Not only so, but even Paul's observation that the God-given law of Moses served to enslave and condemn Israel itself could call into question *Yahweh*'s love for his own people. One result of this seeming conflict has been the conclusion that the OT God is one of wrath while the NT God is one of love (as if, as someone surmised, the NT God had "become a Christian"). This despite the fact that both the old-covenant and the new-covenant scriptures refer to both God's love and God's wrath.

I

While not commonly noted, the theological conundrum (at least in the minds of many thoughtful Bible readers) created by biblical claims regarding God's love, on one hand, and God's wrath on the other, parallels the positive and the negative sides of the Mosaic law. Paul wrote, on one hand, that "the law is holy, and the commandment is holy and righteous and good" (Rom. 7:12) and, on the other hand, that the law "enslaved [God's people] to the elementary principles of the world" (Gal. 4:3). Obviously, Paul's view of the Mosaic law cannot be understood without accounting for both the positive and the negative sides of his assessment. At the same time, accounting for both in biblical terms arguably serves to reconcile the seemingly problematic relationship between God's love and God's wrath.

On the positive side, the Mosaic law is, according to Paul, "holy and righteous and good" (Rom. 7:12) in that it served, and continues to serve, its God-given role. First, the Mosaic law testified to "the righteousness of God" (Rom. 3:21) by calling Israel to obey the ten commandments as the expression of its faith in God's promise to make of Abraham a great nation. Second, the Mosaic law imparted "the knowledge of sin" (Rom. 3:20) to the faithful remnant of Israel by turning Israel's unbelief regarding God's Abrahamic promise into "transgressions" of the ten commandments (Gal. 3:19). Moreover, the Mosaic law still conveys the knowledge of both sin and the righteousness of God through its role in the story of God's Abrahamic promise to bless all nations and its Messianic fulfillment. As such, the Mosaic law is consistent with a God who loves not only Israel but all nations as well.

On the negative side, however, the Mosaic law was misappropriated by dark spiritual forces that turned the law into a system of self-justification, which stood opposed to the righteousness of faith. In so doing, the Mosaic law "enslaved" (Gal. 4:3) God's people, bringing them under "the curse of the law" (Gal. 3:13). Which is to say that the Mosaic law became an instrument of God's wrath – "the law brings wrath" (Rom. 4:15) – condemning God's people for their covenantal unfaithfulness in lieu of justifying them through their faith in God's Abrahamic promise.

According to Paul, Israel's condemnation by the Mosaic law was *not* the work of the God who gave the law through Moses. The critical difference between Paul's positive and negative assessments of the Mosaic law is that, *as an expression of God's wrath, the law was somehow administered by spiritual powers that were hostile to God's purpose.*

That God's law was administered by spiritual powers that were opposed to his purpose suggests a paradox concerning how human beings experience God. On one hand, to experience the love of God through faith in the NT gospel is to experience God as God *is*: "God is love" (John 4:8). On the other hand, to experience the wrath of God – that is, the enslavement and condemnation of law – through unbelief is to experience God as God *is not*. That is to say, to experience the wrath of God is to experience *God in the form of hostile powers which oppose God's purpose.*

What can it mean to experience God in the form of what is not-God and what is opposed to God?

Whatever one worships is, in effect, one's god and, therefore, a representative, whether false or true, of "God": "For although there may be so-called gods in heaven or on earth – as indeed there are many 'gods' and many 'lords' – yet for us there is one God, the Father, from whom are all things and for whom we exist, and one Lord, Jesus Christ, through whom are all things and through whom we exist" (1 Cor. 8:5-6). Which is to say that while Jesus is the true representative of God for believers in the NT gospel, he is by no means the only representative of God in the world.

The biblical God's sovereignty over his creation means that his human creatures must inescapably experience their Creator in one form of representation or another. That the Creator gives his human creatures the freedom to reject his purpose for their lives suggests that their experience of him may then become distorted and misshapen. Perhaps as far from the reality of God as wrath is from love.

II

Paul implied a spiritual distance between God and the Mosaic law in writing that the law "was put in place through angels by an intermediary [literally, 'by the hand of a mediator']. Now [a mediator] implies more than one, but God is one" (Gal. 3:19-20). Just as angelic mediation, in the form of the burning bush through which God spoke to Moses, was instrumental in God's first appearance to Moses (see Exo. 3:2-6), so angels were, according to the tradition from which Paul drew, instrumental in mediating God's giving of the law to Moses at Sinai (see Acts 7:30-32, 53; Heb. 2:2). Both angelic and human (i.e., Moses') mediation were involved, then, in God's giving of the Mosaic law to Israel.

While Paul's reference (in Gal. 3:19-20) to the plurality of mediation as opposed to God's oneness remains obscure (and the subject of scholarly debate), Paul apparently saw the role of angels in the giving of the law as directly related to its temporality, as opposed to the permanence of the promise to Abraham. While God's making of the promise to Abraham was in some sense emblematic of God's oneness – the one God being, ideally, the God of all nations – God's giving of the law to Moses via angelic mediation somehow denoted a more-than-oneness that implied a division between the law and the promise. As Paul asked, "Is the law then contrary to the promises of God?" (Gal. 3:21). While he answered in the negative, the question was nonetheless raised by his reference to angels and mediation in God's giving of the Mosaic law to Israel.

A related idea appears regarding Paul's reference to God's

> having forgiven us all our trespasses, by canceling the record of
> debt that stood against us with its legal demands. This he set aside,
> nailing it to the cross. He disarmed the rulers and authorities
> and put them to open shame, by triumphing over them in him.[1]
> (Col. 2:13-15)

This text connects Jesus' death on the cross for the forgiveness of sins with the Mosaic law, portrayed as both a debt of sin and an instrument of evil angelic powers.

First, forgiveness of sins is the cancellation of a "record of debt" (Greek, *cheirographon*[2]) consisting of "legal demands" (plural form of Greek, *dogma*), a metaphorical reference to the Mosaic law as a legal debt. God has cancelled the legal debt of sin *not by paying it* but by "nailing it to the cross," thus providing forgiveness for "all our trespasses." When the Romans literally nailed Jesus to the cross, then, God was figuratively nailing the Mosaic law to the cross. In so doing, God was cancelling the debt of sin in that the Mosaic law had served as a record of the sins of Israel, calling the nation to account, ever since the giving of the law at Sinai. For Paul, then, *forgiveness of sins was synonymous with the termination of the Mosaic law, which ended the old covenant.*

Secondly, Jesus' crucifixion and the forgiveness of sins is connected to the disarming of "rulers and authorities" (plural forms of Greek, *arche* and *exousia*), which refer to angelic powers arrayed in opposition to God and his Messiah. Paul elsewhere referred to these "rulers and authorities" as "the cosmic powers over this present darkness" and "the spiritual forces of evil in the heavenly places" (Eph. 6:12; see also 1 Cor. 15:24; Eph. 1:21; 2:2; 3:10). These "rulers" and "powers" are associated with "angels" that threatened the spiritual well-being of believers (Rom. 8:38). The existence and activity of

---

[1] Even if, as many scholars believe, Colossians was among the letters written not by Paul himself but by one of his disciples after his death, the letter would, nevertheless, presumably bear witness to Paul's theology.

[2] Literally, handwriting; according to Kittel's *Theological Dictionary of the New Testament*, "A document . . . written in one's own hand as a proof of obligation, e.g., a note of indebtedness."

these hostile "rulers and authorities" (Col. 2:15) corresponds to the tradition, preserved by the NT writers, regarding so-called "fallen angels":

> . . . God did not spare angels when they sinned, but cast them into [*Tartarus*] and committed them to chains of gloomy darkness to be kept until judgment. (2 Pet. 2:4)

> And the angels who did not stay within their own position of authority, but left their proper dwelling, he has kept in eternal chains under gloomy darkness until the judgment of the great day. (Jude 6)

By connecting Jesus' crucifixion and the forgiveness of sins with both the cancelling of the legal debt – that is, the termination of the rule of the Mosaic law over God's people – *and* the disarming of hostile angelic powers, Paul clarified that the Mosaic law had become a weapon of these angelic powers "against" God's people, both enslaving them to sin and condemning them to death. As long as the Mosaic law was in force, then, as the medium of God's rule over his people, they would stand condemned before him. Only, then, by God's bringing the rule of the Mosaic law to an end could God's people experience freedom from its condemnation, that is to say, the forgiveness of sins.

Paul's reference to the Mosaic law being given "through angels" (Gal. 3:19) and to the Mosaic law's having become a weapon of angelic "rulers and authorities" (Col. 2:15) that "stood against" (Col. 2:14) God's people raises at least two questions: First, how did the angelic mediation of the Mosaic law turn into the angelic usurpation of the Mosaic law? And secondly, how could such a development be consistent with the sovereignty of God? The answer to these questions goes a long way toward reconciling the seemingly dissonant biblical testimony regarding the love of God, on one hand, and the wrath of God on the other.

III

The biblical claim that God is sovereign need not mean (Calvinistic theology notwithstanding) that God *causes* all that occurs. But God's sovereignty must mean, nevertheless, that all that occurs is somehow in keeping with God's will. How can this be?

The chief error of Calvinistic theology is its conclusion that God's sovereignty is unalterably opposed to human freedom. According to Calvinism, if God is sovereign, then whatever occurs must be what God predestined, or foreordained, to occur. Accordingly, if an event were to transpire that God did not intend, then God would not be sovereign. Consequently, all that occurs is, in effect, God's doing, whether natural phenomenon or human decision. (And to question God about what occurs is, from the Calvinistic viewpoint, to presume to know better than God how to do his job.)

What if, however, God wills events to run their course according to "time and chance" (Eccl. 9:11) in keeping with the laws of nature, and in that context, God wills humans to be free to choose whether to embrace or reject his purpose? Then both cosmic chance and human choice are part of, and consistent with, God's sovereign will. (And wouldn't the Calvinist who denied this possibility risk presuming to know better than God how to do God's job?)

This does not preclude the biblical claim that God has a sovereign purpose that he predestined from the beginning and that will, therefore, inevitably come to pass. It simply means that God worked out this purpose by intervening in a world otherwise subject to the contingencies of cosmic chance and human choice, as well as controlled and constrained by the invisible laws of nature and human nature. In this way, despite the constraints of human nature – which Paul calls "the law of sin and death" (Rom. 8:2) – humans are nonetheless free to choose whether or not to align themselves with God's purpose (revealed to them through their hearing of God's word about Jesus and the kingdom and grace of God).

If this is the case, the sovereign will of God is necessarily divided into what God *purposes* and what God *permits*.

Accordingly, what God permits is distinct from what God has purposed, that is, has caused, or predestined, to occur. Nevertheless, what God permits is, biblically speaking, as much the will of God as what God has purposed. This is the case because *God wills to permit it*. The difference is that what God purposes is what God desires while what God permits may not be at all what God desires.

Wise human parents permit their growing children an increasing measure of freedom to choose because they desire their children to become mature. As such, their permissive will is a function of their purposive will that their children become free and responsible adults. Nevertheless, permitting their children this increasing measure of freedom inevitably results in their children behaving in ways that their parents neither desire nor approve.

Likewise, God desires human freedom because love, whether for God or neighbor, can only be the exercise of one's freedom to choose. At the same time, God clearly does not desire foolish or hateful exercises of human freedom and the harm that they bring. Nevertheless, God permits his human creatures to exercise their freedom in foolish and hateful ways, though God does not desire it, in order to realize his primary desire – God's purposive will – that human beings grow into the maturity of wisdom and love.

Whether cosmic chance and human choice produce good fortune or misfortune in the earthly affairs of specific persons, both are a matter of God's permissive will. As Jesus said, God "makes his sun rise on the evil and on the good, and sends rain on the just and on the unjust" (Matt. 5:45), which echoes the OT observation that "time and chance happen to them all" (Eccl. 9:11).

By comparison, what God has purposed has disrupted the scenario of both natural law and cosmic chance – via God's miraculous interventions, about which the biblical writers testify – in order to present God's purpose to human choice through the hearing of God's word, giving human beings the opportunity (i.e., the freedom) to align themselves with God's purpose.

If this analysis is accurate, all that has ever occurred and will ever occur is in keeping with God's sovereignty over his creation, whether as a matter of God's *purposive* will – as revealed in the NT gospel of God's Abrahamic promise and its Messianic fulfillment – or of God's *permissive* will, encompassing all else that has ever occurred or will occur until the end of the present age.

In this scenario, the role of "the devil and his angels" (Matt. 25:41, the devil's "angels" otherwise known by the NT writers as "demons") is necessarily played out in terms of God's *permissive* will. God's sovereignty over his creation is expressed not only in his purpose for creation but also in his permission of the spiritual forces of evil to do their work in the present age of sin and death, despite their work being unalterably opposed to God's purpose. Which is to say that the freedom of angels to reject and resist God's purpose is inseparable from the human freedom that is itself integral to God's *purposive* will for his creation.

Accordingly, God works both angelic and human opposition into the fulfillment of his purpose, even as "all things work together for good, for those who are called according to his purpose" (Rom. 8:28). Which is to say that the biblical God's purpose will inevitably come to pass for all who freely choose to align themselves with that purpose, despite the partial angelic and human rejection of that purpose.

This is evidenced by God's use of the Mosaic law's enslavement and condemnation of Israel – engineered, according to Paul, by hostile angelic "rulers and authorities" – to instruct his people in "the knowledge of sin" (Rom. 3:20). And by God's use of the crucifixion of Jesus – clearly engineered by the political and religious establishments under the control of evil angelic powers – to defeat those "rulers and authorities" (Col. 2:15).

The permissive will of God, which allows angelic rulers and authorities as well as their human subjects to reject his purpose and suffer the natural consequences of their choice, is *the biblical meaning of God's wrath*. Paul described "the wrath of God" (Rom. 1:18) on the inhabitants of the present age of sin and death by saying that "God gave them up" (Rom. 1:24, 26, 28) to the consequences of their having "exchanged the truth about God for a lie and worshiped and served the creature rather than the Creator . . ." (Rom. 1:25). *Which is to say that God's wrath is simply God's permission for humanity to reject his purpose and to suffer the natural consequences.*

Chief among the natural consequences of having rejected God's purpose (God's purpose being synonymous with God's covenantal justice; see Chapter 1) is the human need to be ruled by law. Systems of law (i.e., legal justice systems) are a necessity for human social existence because without laws to restrain anti-social behavior, human beings would destroy themselves and one another. Law, then, is biblically speaking, the administrator of God's wrath. Which is to say that God's *permissive* will would lead to the self-destruction of humanity if not for the legal systems of reward and punishment that restrain anti-social behavior. Legal systems work by punishing, that is, *exercising wrath on*, offenders.

As Paul wrote, in regard to the Mosaic law, "the law brings wrath" (Rom. 4:15). In that sense the Mosaic law was like civil law in any society: the ruling authority "is the servant of God, an avenger who carries out wrath on the wrongdoer" (Rom. 13:4). In other words, civil law is "the servant of God" to maintain social order in a world that God has permitted, in the interest of human freedom, to reject his purpose. This does not mean that human administrators of civil law necessarily intend to serve God or that God has any direct dealings with them. It simply means, rather, that human systems of legal justice are the expression of God's wrath (i.e., God's permission to reject his purpose and suffer the natural consequences) in that they are the

God-ordained substitute for God's covenantal justice (see Chapter 1), which is the expression of God's love.

From a biblical standpoint, then, God is sovereign over the universe he created. Therefore, human beings must experience the will of God, insofar as the human creation is accountable to its Creator. Nevertheless, not all human beings will experience God's will in the same way. To experience the *purposive* will of God is to experience God as God *is*: loving, gracious, merciful, forgiving (none of which should be confused with weak). To experience the *permissive* will of God, however, is to experience "God" as God *is not*: wrathful, vengeful, violent, and punitive. In other words, to experience the *permissive* will of God is to experience law, and therefore wrath, instead of love.

Both Israel and the idolatrous nations of the ancient world experienced the *permissive* will, and thus the negative (i.e., the what-God-is-not) side, of God. Under the Mosaic law, which was administered by angelic rulers and authorities which turned out to be hostile to God's purpose, OT Israel experienced the negative side of God, in the form of God's judgments, and Israel often inflicted this negative side of God on its enemies.

The biblical writers identify this activity with God's will, making no distinction between God's *purposive* and God's *permissive* will, because their understanding of God's sovereignty included the activity of these hostile angelic "rulers and authorities" (Col. 2:15). The nations of the ancient world experienced the negative side of God in their worship of those same angelic powers, which were their capricious and blood-thirsty "gods" (which both Moses and Paul identified with "demons": Deut. 32:17; 1 Cor. 10:20-21). They also experienced God's wrath in the form of the arbitrary and punitive laws of their human rulers.

At the same time, in regard to Israel, the God of the Abrahamic promise was always reflected in the call of the Mosaic law for the Israelites to treat one another, as well as resident aliens, as God had treated them by delivering Israel from Egyptian bondage in faithfulness to his promise. And the Abrahamic promise gave Israel hope, even in the midst of God's judgments on the nation for its unfaithfulness, that the nation would be restored to a faithful covenant relationship with its God in God's eschatological kingdom.

And so, the Mosaic law both testified to the righteousness of God and to the unrighteousness of Israel, enslaving and condemning Israel by the power of the spiritual forces of evil. As such, the Mosaic law was the instrument of God, both transmitted through and administered by angelic rulers and authorities. All of these angelic powers were, therefore, God's servants. At the same time, at least some of them were hostile and unwilling servants with their own agenda of violence and oppression. Nevertheless, in God's wisdom, his *purposive* will prevailed by incorporating even the work of "the devil and his angels" – which culminated in the crucifixion of Jesus – into its fulfillment.

Biblically speaking, angels (plural form of Hebrew, *malak*, and Greek, *angelos*, literally, messenger) are God's servants – messengers who both mediate and administer God's purposes in the world. That at least some angels are unwilling servants, whose negative representations of God have even been used by God to fulfill his purpose, seems to be integral to a biblical understanding of the atonement.

IV

The seemingly strange idea that evil angelic powers could serve as the administrators of God's law over, and therefore of God's wrath on, both Israel and the nations finds support in prophetic traditions preserved by both OT and NT writers regarding "Satan" (Greek, *satanas*, literally, adversary).

In the story of Job, Satan is one of "the sons of God" (Job 1:6) – "sons" being a biblical metaphor signifying *agency*, that Satan is one of God's agents, who acts on God's behalf – who challenges God to afflict Job with misfortune. God replies that "all [Job] has is in your hand" (Job 1:12). Which is to say that, in the context of the story itself, when Satan afflicts Job, he does so on God's behalf, as the instrument of God. Afterward, God says to Satan regarding Job, "He still holds fast his integrity, although you incited me against him to destroy him without reason." Despite God's love for Job, Job's experience of God is shaped by Satan and is, therefore, the experience of wrath.

If the story of Job conveys wisdom about God's dealings with his people – and, perhaps, to some extent, with people in general – and not just a person named "Job" (who seems to stand for the righteous person who suffers), then it seems to reveal at least two general truths.

First, the story reveals that earthly misfortune and suffering are not God's punishment for evil-doing (which is the fallacious argument of Job's "comforters," whom God rebukes at the end of the story). Job is, after all, a man whom God commends for his righteousness, which in biblical terms means not legal but covenantal perfection, that is to say, faithfulness.

The second and equally profound truth revealed by the story of Job is that misfortune and suffering are inflicted on human beings not directly by God, as if they were God's *purpose* for certain human beings, but as a matter of God's *permission*.

Just as, in the story, God does not purpose Job's suffering – as if it is predestined before Job was born or a matter of what God desires for Job – so God does not purpose human suffering in general. Nevertheless, God permits it to occur at the hands of Satan, who acts as God's *agent* in the administration of God's wrath. As Job asks his wife, "Shall we receive good from God, and shall we not receive evil?" (Job. 2:10). The wrath of God is the "evil" – signifying not misbehavior but misfortune – that God *permits* in the interest of the human freedom to choose to embrace or reject God's *purpose*.

This is not to say that Satan directly inflicts misfortune and suffering on every human being, whether righteous or wicked, with the acquiescence of God. This would be to take the story of Job too literally, as if Satan must request and receive God's permission to impose affliction in every individual case. Instead, the story reveals the general truth that all misfortune and suffering – whether personal or interpersonal, national or international – occur because Satan is "the god of this age" (2 Cor. 4:4), which is "the present evil age" (Gal. 1:4); the devil is the ruler of "all the kingdoms of the world" (Luke 4:5).

Those who through unbelief experience only the *permissive* will of God, in ignorance of God's purpose, will perceive God, to one extent or another, not as God *is* but as God *is not*. That is to say, they will perceive not the image of the God and Father of Jesus but an image of divinity constructed by the hand of the deceitful "god of this age." The "God" they imagine will be Satanic insofar as he will favor some, for whom he will purpose good fortune, over others, for whom he will purpose misfortune.

And the image of this satanic "God" is reinforced, even magnified, by evangelical Christianity in the form of its rhetoric of the cross. For what could be more Satan-like than a "God" who demands payment for human shortcomings, and whose favor depends on his having been appeased by the life's blood of a divine scapegoat?

The notion of Satan acting as the agent of God's wrath finds further support in the seemingly contradictory OT accounts of King David's census of Israel: "Again the anger of [*Yahweh*] was kindled against Israel, and he incited David against them, saying, 'Go, number Israel and Judah" (2 Sam. 24:1); and "Then Satan stood against Israel and incited David to number

Israel" (1 Chr. 21:1). The unavoidable question: Did *Yahweh* or did Satan incite David to take the census of Israel? Or, were *Yahweh* and Satan one and the same?

The apparent contradiction dissolves with the understanding that Satan acted as God's agent, not in the sense that God ordered Satan to incite David but in the sense that all of Satan's activities are performed with God's *permission*. From the standpoint, therefore, of God's sovereignty (which is invariably the prophetic standpoint of the biblical writers), whatever Satan does *is* an act of God. That God *permitted* the Satanic incitement of an act that was contrary to God's will (a national census being a faithless act to measure and consolidate political power) made it no less an act of God from the prophetic standpoint. Whether done by God according to his *purpose* or by Satan with God's *permission*, all that occurs is a matter of God's sovereign will. And this explains why God's sovereignty is entirely compatible and consistent with the human (as well as the angelic) freedom to choose.

The role of Satan as the devil (Greek, *ho diabolos*, literally, the accuser) is integral to the administration of the Mosaic law by hostile angelic powers and authorities. Just as Satan accuses Job, so in a prophetic vision, Zechariah saw "Joshua the high priest standing before the angel of [*Yahweh*], and Satan standing at his right hand to accuse him" (Zech. 3:1). In the vision, Joshua was "clothed with filthy garments" (Zech. 3:3), signifying the people's transgressions of the Mosaic law, subjecting Joshua, as the people's priestly representative, to Satan's accusations.

The Satanic administration of the Mosaic law for the purpose of accusing God's people is echoed in Jesus' words regarding the effect of his imminent crucifixion: "Now is the judgment of this world; now will the ruler of this world be cast out. And I, when I am lifted up from the earth, will draw all people to myself" (John 12:31-32). Which is to say that Jesus' death on the cross was *for sins* in that its effect was to silence the accusing "ruler of this world," who would no longer be able to use the Mosaic law to accuse God's people of transgression.

Likewise, according to a prophetic vision of the defeat of Satan and his demonic forces at the cross,

> And the great dragon was thrown down, that ancient serpent, who is called the devil and Satan, the deceiver of the whole world – he was thrown down to the earth, and his angels were thrown down with him. And I heard a loud voice in heaven, saying, "Now the

salvation and the power and the kingdom of our God and the
authority of his Christ have come, for the accuser of our brothers
has been thrown down, who accuses them day and night before
our God. And they have conquered him by the blood of the
Lamb . . . ." (Rev. 12:9-11)

In view of "the blood of the Lamb," then, Satan and his angels, in their
capacity as the administrators of God's wrath, can no longer use the Mosaic
law to accuse God's people, enslaving them to sin and condemning them to
death. By "nailing it to the cross" when Jesus was crucified, God "disarmed
the rulers and authorities and put them to open shame, by triumphing over
them in him" (Col. 2:14, 15).

Which is not to say that the angelic "rulers and authorities" do not still
pretend to carry on their administration of the wrath of God via the rule of
the Mosaic law, to whatever degree it continues to be used by Church and
State as the mediator between God and humanity. As Paul wrote, "Satan
disguises himself as an angel of light" (2 Cor. 11:14), and has done so in
the form of a variety of legal systems that have informed the traditions of
Christianity throughout its history. Nevertheless, the termination of the
Mosaic law by means of Jesus' crucifixion means, for those who believe the
NT gospel, both the cancellation of the legal debt of sin and the disarming
of the spiritual forces of evil.

The wrath of God, then, corresponds to the enslaving and condemning
effect of the Mosaic law in the hands of hostile angelic powers, who had a
hand in both the transmission and the administration of the Mosaic law
during the period of its rule over old-covenant Israel. For the NT writers,
deliverance from the wrath of God (i.e., the forgiveness of sins), depended
on the termination of the Mosaic law, which administered God's wrath both
by condemning Israel for its transgressions and by excluding the nations
from covenant relationship with God.

And so, "God shows his love for us in that while we were still sinners,
Christ died for us. Since, therefore, we have now been justified by his
blood, much more shall we be saved by him from the wrath of God" (Rom.
5:8-9).

The question, then, remains: How did the crucifixion of Jesus bring the
rule of the Mosaic law to an end?

CHAPTER 4

The Question of Propitiation

Fundamental to the idea of Jesus' death as payment for sins is the NT use of the term "propitiation" (Rom. 3:25; Heb. 2:17; 1 John 2:2; 4:10). The Greek words typically rendered "propitiation" in English NT versions are *hilasterion* and *hilasmos*. These same words are used by the *Septuagint* (the Greek translation of the Hebrew Old Testament) to translate forms of the Hebrew word *kippur*, which is typically translated "atonement" in English OT versions (as in *Yom Kippur*, Israel's Day of Atonement; see Lev. 23:26-32). Which is to say that "propitiation" and "atonement" are inseparably related in that when sin is atoned for, God is (allegedly) *propitiated*. Atonement and *propitiation* both refer, then, to the payment that God, according to the evangelical rhetoric of the cross, first, *demanded*, due to his justice; second, *provided* – in the form of Jesus' blood – due to his mercy; and third, *accepted*, due to sin's having been atoned for and his having been *propitiated*.

Theopedia, the online *Encyclopedia of Biblical Christianity*, defines *propitiation* as "satisfaction or appeasement, specifically towards God."[i] This evangelical interpretation of *propitiation* directly underlies the notion that God's just demand for payment regarding sins must be *satisfied* in order for sinners to find favor with, that is, to be forgiven by, God.

Simply put, to make atonement, or *propitiation*, is to make payment for sins. *Propitiation* is synonymous with *appeasement* in that it has to do with averting the wrath of God, which is typically understood as God's just, or righteous, reaction to sin. To say that God's justice must be satisfied is to say that God must be *propitiated*, or appeased. The *propitiation* (i.e., atonement/satisfaction/appeasement) *is* the payment. Accordingly, "Propitiation is the work of Jesus Christ on the cross by which He appeases the wrath of God who would otherwise be offended by our sin and demand that we pay the penalty for it."[ii]

Directly associated with NT references to Jesus' death as *propitiation* are OT references to the animal sacrifices prescribed by the Mosaic law. Under the law, the place of *propitiation*, or atonement, on the ark of the covenant, was called "the mercy seat" (Exo. 25:17-18, translated by the Greek *hilasterion* in Heb. 9:5) and was sprinkled with the blood of animal sacrifices on the Day of Atonement. According to the NT writers, these sacrifices prefigured the crucifixion of Jesus. Therefore, as the evangelical theory of the atonement infers, "The thought in the Old Testament sacrifices and in the New Testament fulfillment is that Christ completely satisfied the just demands of a holy God for judgment on sin by His death on the Cross."[iii]

To be clear, then, the picture of God projected by the evangelical rhetoric of the cross is of a deity whose sense of "justice" calls forth wrath on those who offend him by transgressing his law, necessitating that he demand payment from them. This payment must take the form of either the damnation of the souls of the transgressors themselves *or* the lifeblood of a sinless substitute. This sinless substitute, according to the evangelical doctrine, God not only demanded but also provided and accepted, thereby permitting himself to "forgive" transgressors. Which is simply and clearly to say that God's forgiveness had to be legally justified by Jesus' crucifixion. And this can only, if plain language means what it says, mean that God's forgiveness could not be freely given. That is, God could not forgive purely as a matter of grace.

I

The notion of a payment demanded in order to appease a wrathful God has been problematic for many theologians as well as for many thoughtful Christians.

First, the idea of appeasement makes the biblical God look much like the pagan gods of the ancient world whose worshipers unapologetically understood their sacrifices as a way of paying off their gods. They sought to buy the gods' favor out of abject fear of the gods' displeasure.

Second, the idea of appeasement makes the biblical God look far too human, reflecting the worst rather than the best features of human nature:

a personal offense leads one to feel anger, which leads one to demand, or at least expect, some form of payment – an effort to "make up for it" – as a condition of foregoing some form of revenge (which may range from the silent treatment to physical violence).

Naturally, apologists for the evangelical doctrine are quick to deny the parallel: "Propitiation is not the placating of a vengeful God but, rather, it is the satisfying the righteousness of a holy God, thereby making it possible for Him to show mercy without compromising His righteousness or justice."[iv]

What is the difference, however, between "satisfying the righteousness of a holy God" and "placating a vengeful God"? Is there a difference, in this rhetorical construct, between "satisfying" and "placating"? Between "a holy God" and "a vengeful God"? If God's holiness requires that he take vengeance on those who offend him, then there is no difference. The notion of requiring payment for an offense is, by definition, vengeance. The alternative is forgiveness, which means cancelling the debt *rather than* demanding payment for it.

That it is God's "justice" that supposedly demands the payment does not alter the picture of *propitiation* as "the placating of a vengeful God." This God remains unforgiving *unless he is propitiated*, that is to say, *paid to forgive*. But this means that this God is, in fact, incapable of forgiveness. At least as long as forgiveness is, by definition, the cancellation of an *unpaid* debt. The notion that the evangelical God *propitiates himself* in the person of his Son – who in Trinitarian terms is part of Godself – does not alter the portrayal of a God who cannot forgive without payment. Which is, then, to say that this God cannot forgive at all.

The understandable discomfort of theologians with the portrayal of God as a vengeful deity who must be appeased in order for his worshipers to experience his favor has led some to insist that a better translation of the relevant NT Greek words (*hilasmos* and *hilasterion*) than "propitiation" is "expiation" (which some NT English versions employ). The difference, according to *Theopedia*, is that the meaning of *propitiation* is "to *make favorable* and specifically includes the idea of dealing with God's wrath against sinners," whereas the meaning of *expiation* is "to *make pious* and implies either the removal or cleansing of sin [but has] no reference to quenching God's righteous anger. The difference is that the object of expiation is sin, not God. One propitiates a person, and one expiates a problem."[v] Translating the Greek terms as "expiation" rather than "propitiation" is an effort to circumvent the pagan (which also continues to be the evangelical) idea of "the placating of a vengeful God."

Nevertheless, the substitution of "expiation" for "propitiation" raises the question of why it would be necessary for Jesus to die on the cross in order to *expiate*, or remove, sin unless God required it. If God's justice/righteousness required – and therefore God demanded – the death of Jesus as payment in order to *expiate* sin, then the element of *propitiation* seems inescapable. The *expiation* of sin must require the *propitiation* of God. Consequently, *propitiation* – the idea of Jesus' death as payment – seems to be an unavoidable element in any NT theory of the atonement.

II

The NT writers did indeed call Jesus' death a *propitiation*. But if the biblical "God is love" (1 John 4:8), then the notion that he demanded payment in order to extend forgiveness is both logical and theological nonsense. God-given reason demands another interpretation of Jesus' *death-as-propitiation*.

The evangelical doctrine that God must pay himself to forgive makes the forgiveness of sins a *divine transaction* carried out within the evangelical "Godhead": God-the-Father demanding payment, then providing payment to Godself in the form of the crucified God-the-Son, then accepting the payment of blood from the resurrected Son, and only then dispensing forgiveness in the form of God-the-Holy-Spirit.

The stark contrast between the evangelical *atonement-as-transaction* and the NT *atonement-as-gift* exposes the evangelical doctrine as not merely absurd but thoroughly heinous. The evangelical appeal that it was God himself who provided himself with the payment in no way mitigates the appalling claim – which the NT writers themselves never made – that God demanded payment as a condition of forgiving sinners.

Nevertheless, Jesus' crucifixion was "a propitiation . . . to show God's righteousness" (Rom. 3:25), through which God provided the forgiveness of sins to all who believe the NT gospel. But Jesus died as a *propitiation* not only "to show God's righteousness" but also, somehow, as the ultimate illustration of God's love: "In this is love, not that we have loved God but that he loved us and sent his Son to be the propitiation for our sins" (1 John 4:10).

The evangelical explanation is that Jesus' *death-as-propitiation* shows God's justice in that *God's justice demanded* Jesus' blood-as-payment. And that Jesus' *death-as-propitiation* shows God's love in that *God's love provided* Jesus' blood-as-payment. But this reasoning is purely inferential in that the NT writers gave no such explanation.

Moreover, it calls the mental and emotional health of this God into question: A human being created in the image of this God would arguably be diagnosed as schizophrenic if he or she indignantly issued a demand for payment of a debt in one breath, and then, in the next breath, pronounced the debt forgiven after having accepted that payment from his or her own hand. (Which also explains why evangelical Christianity is so able to unselfconsciously employ, in equal parts, the inspirational rhetoric of forgiveness and acceptance, on one hand, and the judgmental rhetoric of exclusion and coercion, on the other. Evangelical rhetoric often reflects the tortured soul of its two-faced God.)

By comparison, the NT writers naturally combined the idea of *propitiation* – the payment made to a wrathful deity – with the idea of God's unconditional love, absent any of the theological gymnastics performed by the evangelical rhetoric of the cross to harmonize God's justice with God's mercy, God's wrath with God's love. This can only be because the NT writers, like the best of their OT predecessors, knew the God of Israel and of Israel's Messiah to be a God of promise rather than a God of law. Only when God's justice/righteousness is understood in *covenantal* rather than in *legal* terms (see Chapter 1), and only when God's law is understood as the instrument of evil angelic powers who administer God's wrath (see Chapter 3), do the otherwise seemingly logical and theological contradictions in the NT language of the atonement disappear.

When God's justice/righteousness is understood in *covenantal* terms – that is, as God's faithfulness to his Abrahamic promise – then Jesus' death on the cross clearly "show[s] God's righteousness" (Rom. 3:25), not in the sense that it satisfies the demand of God for payment of the legal debt of sin but in the sense that it terminates the Mosaic law – the angelic usurpation of which being the true source of the demand for payment – in order to fulfill the promise of God to bless all nations.

In view of Jesus' crucifixion, God is "just" – that is, faithful to his promise – as well as "the justifier" of believers in the promise (Rom. 3:26). God does not justify believers *despite* their not being perfectly obedient to the Mosaic law, as if God *would have* justified them if they had been perfectly obedient. This evangelical notion assumes that righteousness *could* have been earned by law-keeping. Instead, God justifies believers for the same reason that he justified Abraham, who "believed God, and it was counted to him as righteousness" (Rom. 4:3; Gal. 3:6; Gen. 15:6). That is, believers' faith – the faith of Jesus himself in God's Abrahamic promise – is "counted to [them] as righteousness."

God justified Jesus, not because Jesus was perfectly obedient to the Mosaic law but because Jesus believed God's Abrahamic promise to bless all nations in Abraham's seed. According to the NT writers, this in Jesus' exclusive case meant believing God's revelation to him that he himself was Abraham's Messianic seed. Jesus' faith in God's promise led him to his crucifixion, and God justified him by raising him from the dead. So it is that God is "the justifier of the one who has [the faith of] Jesus"[1] (Rom. 3:26). That is, God justifies (counts as righteous) the one who believes the same promise that Jesus – and his ancestor Abraham before him – believed.

Regarding the commandments to love God with one's entire being and to love one's neighbor as oneself, Jesus announced, "On these two commandments depend all the Law and the Prophets" (Matt. 22:40). His words imply why he seems not to have busied himself with the legal regulations and ceremonies of the Mosaic law, not to mention his disregard for the so-called "tradition of the elders" (Matt. 15:2), the legal hedge that the Pharisees had built around the law ostensibly to ensure its observance. Jesus' love for his neighbors manifested for all to see his faith in and faithfulness to – that is to say, his love for – the God of promise.

All of which is to say that, through the NT gospel, "the righteousness of God has been manifested *apart from the law* [being] the righteousness

---

[1]   . Pauline texts that refer to the "faith of" Jesus, rather than (as typically translated) "faith in" Jesus, include Rom. 3:22, 26; Gal. 2:16 (twice); 3:22; and Phil. 3:9. While either translation is permissible in the original language, the linguistic construction in each case is identical to the reference of Rom. 4:16 to "the faith of Abraham," which clearly cannot be understood as "faith in Abraham." Moreover, in each text, including Rom. 4:16, the subject is "righteousness" as a matter of faith: just as righteousness came to Abraham, and through Abraham to his descendents, through Abraham's faith, so righteousness came to Jesus, and comes through Jesus to believers, through Jesus' faith. The Trinitarian notion that Jesus was God-in-the-flesh and, therefore, could not have needed faith may be largely responsible for the penchant of English NT versions to favor the objective genitive rendering "faith in" over the subjective genitive rendering "faith of."

of God through [the faith of Jesus Christ] for all who believe" (Rom. 3:21, 22). God's *justice*, then, is a matter not of *law and payment* but of *promise and fulfillment*.

Likewise, when God's Mosaic law is understood as the instrument of evil angelic powers who administer God's wrath (see Chapter 3), only then is it clear that Jesus' blood did not *propitiate* God, as if God had to be paid to forgive sins. Instead, the "propitiation by his blood" (Rom. 3:25) is that which "disarmed the rulers and authorities" (Col. 2:15), who could no longer, in view of Jesus' death for sins, use the law to condemn God's people.

Jesus suffered the full condemnation of the Mosaic law on the cross, paying the legal debt in full, God thereby "canceling the record of debt that stood against us with its legal demands . . . , nailing it to the cross" (Col. 2:14b). In this text, the Mosaic law is metaphorically portrayed as the "debt" that God cancelled by "nailing it to the cross," thereby "having forgiven us all our trespasses" (Col. 2:14a). *The termination of the rule of the Mosaic law over God's people is the NT meaning of the forgiveness of sins.*

But if Jesus' crucifixion represented both his *payment* of the legal debt and God's *cancellation* of the legal debt – which can only qualify as *forgiveness* in the absence of payment – then it cannot be God who either demanded or received the payment.

The Mosaic law itself demanded payment for sins, placing "all who rely on works of the law . . . under a curse; for it is written, 'Cursed be everyone who does not abide by all things written in the Book of the Law, and do them'" (Gal. 3:10). All who tried to justify themselves through their observance of the Mosaic law were cursed – "all who rely on works of the law are under a curse" – because "they did not pursue [righteousness] by faith, but as if it were based on works" (Rom. 9:32). The problem was that the Mosaic law, through its condemnation of transgressors, compelled them – as slaves are compelled – to seek to justify themselves by their "works of the law."

This was, then, the effect of the evil angelic administration of the Mosaic law: the subversion of the Mosaic law *from* being an instrument for the expression of faith in the Abrahamic promise *into* a system of self-justification, placing Israel "under a curse."

Despite the *spiritual ideal* of the Mosaic law as an instrument of faith in the Abrahamic promise, the Israelite use of the law as an instrument of self-justification (illustrated by the NT Gospels' portrayal of the Pharisees) was the *religious reality*: "But the law is not of faith, rather 'The one who does them shall live by them'" (Gal. 3:12). Both the angelic transmission and the angelic usurpation of the Mosaic law meant that the effect of the law on God's people would be not the righteousness of faith but the enslavement and condemnation of self-justification. And so, as long as God's people remained under the Mosaic law, they would remain "under a curse."

III

So, "Christ redeemed us from the curse of the law by becoming a curse for us – for it is written, 'Cursed is everyone who is hanged on a tree'" (Gal. 3:13). The only way for the biblical God's people to be "redeemed [Greek, *exagorazo*: freed by means of purchase] from the curse of the law" was for the rule of the Mosaic law to be brought to an end.

Both *redemption* and *propitiation* are payment-terms. While *propitiation* refers to the payment made to appease an angry god, *redemption* refers to the payment made to release slaves from bondage. Both terms are metaphors that the NT writers used to convey to their readers what the effect of the crucifixion of Jesus *is like* in terms with which they were familiar. (Both the *propitiation* of gods and the *redemption* of slaves were part of the general experience and observation of life in the ancient world.) The effect of Jesus' crucifixion *is like a propitiation*, or appeasement, of a wrathful god, whose anger now turns to favor. The effect of the cross *is like a redemption* of slaves, who have been set free from their master.

The evangelical error is to literalize these metaphors, as if the God and Father of Jesus is *literally* propitiated by Jesus' blood. To be consistent, however, literalizing the metaphor of *propitiation* requires literalizing the metaphor of *redemption*. Which is to say that it requires believing that Jesus' blood was offered as payment to . . . Whom? Or to what? Did God, in the person of Jesus, offer Jesus' blood to sin, to which sinners are enslaved? Or to the Mosaic law, to which God's people were enslaved under the old covenant? Or to Satan, "the god of this age" (2 Cor. 4:4), who rules over the slaves of sin? The notion that God would be obligated to make a payment to his own law, or worse, to make a payment to sin, or worse still, to make a payment to Satan, is too outrageous for even evangelical theology to entertain.

Just as *the master* from whose ownership the slaves are *redeemed* by the payment cannot be the biblical God, so neither can *the god* who is *propitiated* by the payment be the biblical God. In each case, whether of *redemption* or *propitiation*, the recipient of the payment must be the same party.

And so it is: both *the god* and *the master* are metaphors that represent *what the Mosaic law was like* in terms of its effect on God's old-covenant people. Which is to say that the Mosaic law is personified by the NT writers as *a god* and as *a master*, each demanding payment. Just as *the master must be paid* – as in compensated – before he will free his slaves, so *the god must be paid* – as in appeased – to turn his anger to favor.

The *payment-as-redemption* results in freedom from the master. The Mosaic law "enslaved [God's people] to the elementary principles of the world" (Gal. 4:3), from which God's people are now free, having been "released from the law, having died to what held us captive, so that we serve not under the old written code but in the new life of the Spirit" (Rom. 7:6).

The *payment-as-propitiation* results in the favor of the god. The Mosaic law had brought condemnation on Israel due to Israel's unbelief: "the law brings wrath" (Rom. 4:15). The Mosaic law now shows favor to God's people by bearing witness to "the righteousness of God" (Rom. 3:21) through its biblical role in the story of God's Abrahamic promise and its Messianic fulfillment.

IV

The most significant, and egregious, error of the evangelical doctrine of the atonement is that it locates the barrier between God and the human world in the heart of God. *The evangelical God could not find it in his heart to forgive and accept sinners apart from a payment that justified his doing so.* This God had to be *propitiated* – appeased, placated, satisfied, pacified – before he could accept sinners (which, to repeat perhaps *ad nauseum*, should not be confused with forgiveness). And because humanity could not *propitiate* this God, he had to *propitiate* himself in order to remove the barrier that stood between himself and his human creatures.

By comparison, the biblical writers locate the barrier between God and humanity squarely in the human heart: "The heart is deceitful above all things, and desperately sick; who can understand it?" (Jer. 17:9); "They are darkened in their understanding, alienated from the life of God because of the ignorance that is in them, due to their hardness of heart" (Eph. 4:18).

The problem that has been solved by Jesus' *death-as-propitiation*, then, is not the inability of the biblical God to forgive without payment. Payment was required, rather, to persuade hearts hardened by both sin and law to open themselves to God's love – to the full assurance of God's acceptance. While human beings can pay lip service to the love of God, it is simply not within their power to soften their own hearts so as to open themselves to a God they cannot see – as in perceive directly – and whose image has been obscured and distorted by the dark lords of religious authority throughout human history.

For the objective hope of resurrection from death to everlasting life in the kingdom of God to become a matter of subjective assurance, the fear of punishment, which is the only motivation that religious authority can instill in human hearts, must be replaced by the love of God: "There is no fear in love, but perfect love casts out fear. For fear has to do with punishment, and whoever fears has not been perfected in love" (1 John 4:18).

The NT gospel offers the death of Jesus on the cross as the persuasive evidence of God's love for one and all, here and now, each time it is proclaimed: "God *shows* his love for us in that while we were still sinners, Christ died for us" (Rom. 5:8).

As such, Jesus' *death-as-propitiation* supplies "confidence" to doubtful believers that God views them not as transgressors of his law but as children of his love:

> Therefore, brothers, since we have confidence to enter the holy
> places by the blood of Jesus, by a new and living way that he
> opened for us through the curtain, that is, through his flesh,
> and since we have a great priest over the house of God, let us
> draw near with a true heart in full assurance of faith, with our
> hearts sprinkled clean from an evil conscience and our bodies
> washed with pure water. Let us hold fast the confession of our
> hope without wavering, for he who promised is faithful. (Heb.
> 10:19-23)

The NT term "reconciliation" (Rom. 5:11; 2 Cor. 5:18-19) refers not to any change in the heart of God toward the world brought about by the crucifixion of Jesus but to the change in human hearts that have been persuaded by the biblical message that the biblical God is for them rather than against them:

> If God is for us, who can be against us? He who did not spare his
> own Son but gave him up for us all, how will he not also with him
> graciously give us all things? Who shall bring any charge against

God's elect? It is God who justifies. Who is to condemn? Christ
Jesus is the one who died – more than that, who was raised – who
is at the right hand of God, who indeed is interceding for us.
(Rom. 8:31-34)

While, for the NT writers, human beings are unknowingly "enemies" of
God in the sense that they are "alienated from the life of God because of
the ignorance that is in them, due to their hardness of heart" (Eph. 4:18),
God has never been the enemy of humanity:

> For if while we were enemies we were reconciled to God by the
> death of his Son, much more, now that we are reconciled, shall
> we be saved by his life. More than that, we also rejoice in God
> through our Lord Jesus Christ, through whom we have now
> received reconciliation. (Rom. 5:10-11)

The NT relationship between *propitiation* and *reconciliation* is critical
to an understanding of the atonement.

If (as evangelical Christianity insists) God was *propitiated*, his anger
turned to favor, by the death of Jesus, then God was an enemy of the world,
due to its sin, and was, due to Jesus' *death-as-propitiation*, thereby *reconciled*
to the world. And only then could God accept sinners who turned to him
in faith.

But the NT writers nowhere say that God *was reconciled*, or that God
reconciled himself, to the world by Jesus' *death-as-propitiation*, as if God were
ever alienated from human beings in the first place.

Instead, Paul wrote that "in Christ God was reconciling the world to
himself, not counting their trespasses against them" (2 Cor. 5:19).

The purpose of the *propitiation*, then, was *not* to *reconcile* God to the
world but *to persuade the world to be reconciled to God*: "We implore you on
behalf of Christ, be reconciled to God" (2 Cor. 5:20). This is the persuasive
appeal of the NT *logos* [2] not only to professing believers but also to the rest

---

[2]   The Greek word *logos* is typically translated "word," in the sense of message,
by NT English versions. It came originally not from the world of religion but
from the world of rhetoric, being central to the art of persuasion that arose in
ancient Greece. In its original rhetorical context, *logos* referred to *speech as the
combination of reason and persuasion*. The NT writers used *logos* with primary

of the world: "He is the propitiation for our sins, and not for ours only but also for the sins of the whole world" (1 John 2:2). The biblical God's forgiveness, then, is freely extended to all through the NT message, and *reconciliation* is experienced by those who believe and, therefore, receive God's forgiveness.

V

The self-concept of every first-century Jew and the national identity of the Jewish people was deeply and firmly rooted in the Mosaic law and inseparable from adherence to it. What would it take to persuade first-century Jews, then, that the work of the Mosaic law was done and that it would no longer mediate their relationship to their God? That the Mosaic law, which had become "a yoke . . . that neither our fathers nor we have been able to bear" (Acts 15:10), could no longer condemn them for their individual transgressions or their national history of unfaithfulness?

Due to the Babylonian conquest of Judah in the sixth century B.C.E., and the subsequent exile and dispersion of Jews – and Jewish communities of faith – all over the ancient world, virtually every first-century Gentile's understanding of the Hebrew God and his people was equally inseparable from the Mosaic law. The Hebrew God was the God of the Mosaic law, and the people of this God seemed to have used the law to condemn and exclude the idolatrous nations, reminding Gentiles that they were "alienated from the commonwealth of Israel and strangers to the covenants of promise, having no hope and without God in the world" (Eph. 2:12). What would it take to persuade first-century Gentiles, then, that they could now identify themselves with and embrace the faith of the people of the Hebrew God without reference to the Mosaic law? That the law no longer stood between them and the Hebrew God and his people?

---

reference to the NT gospel, the message that the NT Jesus persuaded his disciples to believe and with which he entrusted them to persuade all nations. As a *logos*, the NT gospel appealed to its hearers' rationality with claims supported by the evidence of eyewitness testimony, rather than appealing to their religious superstitions. The contrasting linguistic counterpart of *logos* from the world of religion was the word *mythos*, from which comes the English word that combines *logos* and *mythos*: mythology, or the study of ancient religions.

In sum, what would it take to persuade one and all that the justifying rule of the Messianic faith had come to replace the condemning rule of the Mosaic law? And that the Messiah had come to bless not only the nation of the law but all the nations of the earth?

Insofar as the curse of the Mosaic law could only be removed by the blood of transgressors, "God put forward" his Son, the promised Messiah of Israel, "as a propitiation by his blood, to be received by faith" (Rom. 3:25).

To ask who received the payment of Jesus' blood, if not God himself, is to press the metaphor of *propitiation* too far. The Mosaic law itself, under the influence of the angelic powers of darknesss, was the metaphorical *god* who demanded the payment, but God was obviously under no obligation to offer the blood of his Son to his own law – much less to the devil, who had usurped its authority – in order to bring the law's condemning rule to an end. (According to Gustaf Aulen, that the payment of Jesus' blood was made to Satan was a widespread belief among Christians between the post-apostolic period and the middle ages, when Anselm's legal theory that made God himself the recipient of his own payment became the orthodox doctrine.)

No recipient need be identified for a metaphorical payment. The purpose of the *propitiation* was not literally to pay off anything or anyone so that forgiveness could somehow be justified. The fact is that forgiveness can never be justified in any legal sense. It can only and ever be freely given, an act of extravagant generosity.

Rather, the purpose of the *propitiation*, as far as the NT writers were concerned, was purely rhetorical: to persuade human hearts that the gates of the coming kingdom of God were wide open and that all from every nation were welcome therein and invited to prepare for its arrival.

Endnotes

i.   "Propitiation." *Theopedia: An Encyclopedia of Biblical Christianity.* <*www.theopedia.com/Propitiation*>.

ii.   Ibid.

iii. Ibid.

iv. Ibid.

v.   Ibid.

CHAPTER 5

The Question of Forgiveness

The oft-repeated premise of this book is that God cannot both have demanded, provided and accepted payment for sins, on one hand, *and* have forgiven sins on the other. This is, once again, because forgiveness is, by definition, the cancellation of an *unpaid* debt. Once the debt is paid, then, it can no longer be forgiven.

This is both a logical and a theological argument. If, logically speaking, God cannot both accept payment for sins *and* forgive sins, then theologically speaking, a God whose nature somehow demanded or allowed him to do so could hardly be a God who endowed his human creatures with rationality. This could not be the God who cries out to his people, "Come now, let us reason together" (Isa. 1:18, which *Yahweh* says in regard to the forgiveness of his people's sins). Theology is, after all, the application of reason (Greek, *logos*) to the understanding of God (Greek, *theos*).

I

The logical dilemma for those who would apply their God-given reason to the biblical testimony about Jesus' crucifixion is to understand why the NT writers claim, on one hand, that Jesus *paid the debt* of sin and, on the other hand, that God *forgave the debt* of sin. Thus the logical, and theological, question: How can God have cancelled an *unpaid* debt – which God would have had to do to have forgiven it – if Jesus, at God's direction, paid the debt?

The solution to this logical problem depends on understanding "forgiveness" as a *figurative comparison to* rather than as a *literal description of* the effect of Jesus' crucifixion.

The central argument of this book is that, according to the NT writers, the literal effect of Jesus' crucifixion was the termination of the national covenant between the biblical God and Israel. Before the *international covenant* between God and all nations could begin, the *national covenant* between God and the nation of Israel had to come to an end. The termination of the national covenant meant the termination of the Mosaic law as the biblical God's means of ruling his people. This is the NT meaning of the forgiveness of sins: "God made us alive together with him, having forgiven us all our trespasses, by canceling the record of debt that stood against us with its legal demands. This he set aside, nailing it to the cross" (Col. 2:14).

Forgiveness is a *figurative comparison* in that the termination of the Mosaic law *is like* the cancellation of an unpaid debt. God's people could only pay their legal debt, satisfying the demand of the Mosaic law, by suffering the punishment of "death" (Deut. 30:15); as Paul wrote, "the letter kills" (2 Cor. 3:6). By terminating the rule of the Mosaic law, which was *like* a debt in that it held God's people accountable for their transgressions, God refused to make his people pay their legal debt: God cancelled the debt by terminating the rule of the Mosaic law.

The term "forgiveness," then, refers *literally* to the cancellation of a financial debt, but as used by the NT writers, "forgiveness" refers *figuratively* to the cancellation of the figurative, legal debt represented by the Mosaic law.

But this can have nothing literally to do with forgiveness in the commonly understood sense of a change of heart, or attitude, within an offended party toward an offender. In other words, God's forgiveness of sins occurred externally to God, and historically, rather than occurring internally to God and continuously, every time a sinner repents. For if forgiveness occurs – and, therefore, continually must occur – internally, that is, in the heart of God, then God's forgiveness necessitated – and necessitates, every time it occurs – a change of God's attitude toward a sinner: from resentment and alienation to acceptance and reconciliation.

To think of God's forgiveness as occurring within God's heart every time a sinner repents – which is surely the popular concept of God's forgiveness – is to miss the biblical sense of forgiveness altogether. The biblical sense assumes the literal meaning of forgiveness as the cancellation of an unpaid *financial* debt and applies it figuratively to the termination of the Mosaic law, as the cancellation of the unpaid *legal* debt of Israel. The evangelical sense of forgiveness, however, misses both the literal sense and its figurative application as employed by the NT writers, substituting for it the commonly understood *moral* sense of forgiveness. This sense of forgiveness assumes a *moral* debt of sin that sinners owe to God himself, whose wrath must then be understood in terms of his resentment toward and alienation from sinners. Accordingly, forgiveness of sins must be understood as God's *change-of-heart-toward-sinners*, supposedly *Self-induced*: That is, God's *forgiveness-as-change-of-heart-toward-sinners* is ostensibly brought about by a payment made by God-the-Son to God-the-Father.

The evangelical rhetoric of the cross not only substitutes a *moral* sense of forgiveness for the *literal-financial/figurative-legal* sense employed by the NT writers, but it also maligns the holiness of God. That God is "holy" (Greek, *hagios*) means that God is *set apart* – that is, different – from the gods of the nations and, therefore, from the unbelieving world that worships them. But the biblical God is not different from the gods, or the humans who worship them, if he holds offenses against the offenders and must be appeased by human sacrifice in order to show them favor.

Christianity (as opposed to the NT writers) has historically defined God's holiness, just like his forgiveness, in *moral* terms. This definition, which has become the popular understanding, of God's holiness is *God's intolerance of human imperfection*. Evangelical Christianity has continued to construe the biblical God as a righteously indignant Moralist who burns with rage toward "sin" – defined as *moral-legal* imperfection – and therefore must, like Shakespeare's Shylock, demand his pound of flesh for every human imperfection. Nevertheless, while hating the sin, this God supposedly loves the sinner. The only way, then, to *feel* about "forgiveness of sins" in the face of the evangelical God is that one has been *let off the hook*, while *the hook* itself (the law) remains. That such a "forgiveness" could engender assurance about God's love in believing hearts seems highly unlikely.

The biblical God, however, is not like human beings insofar as being prone to resentment and retaliation when wronged. In other words, "forgiveness of sins" does not refer to a change of God's attitude toward sinners, from resentment and alienation *via* forgiveness to acceptance and reconciliation, as the *moral* sense of "forgiveness" signifies in human relationships.

The *moral* sense of forgiveness can be outlined in terms of a process: *first*, one *wrongs* (i.e., offends) another; *second*, the wronged party *resents* the offender and is, therefore, *alienated from* the offender; *third*, the wronged party *forgives* the offender and is, therefore, *reconciled to* the offender, and the offender is, as a result, *reconciled* to the one he or she has wronged.

The *third* step in this process – the wronged party *forgives* the offender and is, therefore, *reconciled to* the offender – is *the giving up and letting go of the resentment* the wronged party feels toward the offender. The *moral* debt is cancelled in the sense that *resentment against* the offender, resulting in *alienation from* the offender, is replaced by *acceptance* of the offender, resulting in *reconciliation to* the offender. The *moral* application of the forgiveness-metaphor to human relationships, then, assumes that the wronged party feels *resentment* in his or her heart *against* and, therefore, *alienation from* the offender.

This being the case, God would have to experience resentment in his heart against sinners and alienation from them in order to forgive them in this *moral* sense. But this is precisely what the NT writers never say about the biblical God: that God was, or is, *alienated from* sinners, and was or is, through the atonement of Christ, *reconciled to* them (see Chapter 4).

In fact, what the NT writers say that precludes the possibility of God's *alienation from* and *reconciliation to* sinners is, in the words of John, that "God is love" (1 John 4:8). More specifically, as Paul wrote, love is "not . . . resentful" (1 Cor. 13:5). The phrase "not . . . resentful" (ESV) is alternatively rendered "does not take into account a wrong *suffered*" (NASB, italics indicating that no word in the original language corresponds to "suffered") and "keeps no record of wrongs" (NIV). The literal rendering of the original language is *does not reckon the evil*. All of which is to say that one who loves *refuses to hold an offense against the offender*. Refuses, that is, to view the offender as a debtor, as one who owes payment for the offense.

The logic of love is, therefore, inescapable: If "God is love," then God refuses to hold the sins of sinners against them. *Which is to say that there is no moral debt of sin.* The biblical God is not a debt holder who must relate to human beings as transgressors, that is, as debtors. God holds no *moral* debt that he must cancel – that is, forgive – before he can relate to his human creatures as beloved persons rather than as transgressors of law. While the biblical God's human creatures are clearly alienated from God by their sin – that is, their unbelief toward God manifested in the worship of other gods – God has never been alienated from his human creatures.

Obviously, a relationship requires that neither party be alienated from the other. But the biblical point is that the obstacle to the relationship between God and human beings is not on God's side, in God's heart, but on the human side, in the human heart, whether or not human beings are conscious of this alienation.

All of which is to say, again, that the NT forgiveness of sins cannot occur in the heart of God, wherein he cancels a moral debt whenever a sinner repents, ostensibly because God *pre-paid* himself with the blood of Christ to do so. Instead, the NT forgiveness of sins occurred externally to God, historically – "once for all" (Heb. 9:12, 26) – at the cross, cancelling once and for all the legal debt of the Mosaic law, so that thereafter "repentance and the forgiveness of sins should be proclaimed to all nations" (Luke 24:47).

That God held no *moral* debt against sinners in his heart that he had to forgive before he could accept them explains why the Jesus of the NT Gospels relates to "the tax collectors and sinners" not as God-forsaken transgressors – as did the Pharisees – but as persons who, because of their creation in God's image, were worthy of their Creator's love.

That it is not the biblical God but, rather, the Mosaic law that held sins against sinners is clear in that "sin is not counted where there is no law" (Rom. 5:13). Between God's creation of Adam and God's giving of the law through Moses, then, sin was "not counted." The word rendered "counted" is a form of the same word as *reckon* in 1 Corinthians 13:5 (Greek, *ellogeo*, literally, "to charge to an account"[i]). Because *God-as-love does not reckon* (i.e., count) *the evil*, "sin is not counted where there is no law."

That it was "not counted" before the Mosaic law does not mean that sin did not alienate the world from God; it means, rather, that the world remained ignorant of its alienation from God. Paul's point is that sin – unbelief-manifested-in-the-worship-of-other-gods – exists without reference to law, but sin is *reckoned* or *counted*, as in *charged to an account*, when law is applied to it (Gal. 3:19). Law becomes an account of law-breakers' transgressions against it, making them conscious of guilt and, therefore, fearful of punishment. Once the Mosaic law was "added" to the Abrahamic promise, sin took the form of "transgressions" (Gal. 3:19), which testified to Israel's unfaithfulness toward – and, therefore, alienation from – its God, becoming the figurative *debt* that enslaved Israel to its condemning rule (see Chapter 2).

The Mosaic law was able to make Israel aware of its alienation from God – conveying "the knowledge of sin" (Rom. 3:20) – by ensuring that Israel's unbelief-manifested-in-idolatry "counted" as sin by taking the form of transgression, the first commandment being, "You shall have no other gods *besides* me" (Exo. 20:3, *besides* being the preferable rendering to "before"). The literal meaning of *sin* (Greek, *hamartia*) is *missing the mark*, the *mark* being not the Mosaic law but God himself: sin as unbelief-manifested-in-the-worship-of-other-gods means, for the biblical writers, *missing God* and, therefore, *the hope of life*. The Mosaic law not only made Israel aware of its alienation from God but also locked Israel into that alienation, being unable to effect reconciliation and, therefore, locking all nations out of the possibility of reconciliation (see Gal. 3:21-23).

In sum, because God does not charge sin to the account of sinners, as did the Mosaic law, then it does not make sense to say that God forgives sinners in the *moral* sense of giving up resentment against them and becoming reconciled to them. And, in fact, the NT writers say *not* that God is reconciled to the world *but* that *God reconciled the world to himself* in Christ (see Chapter 4).

The biblical wrath of God (see Chapter 3) is not God's feeling of resentment or attitude of rejection toward sinners. God's wrath is, instead, *the effect of their alienation from God on them*, specifically, their need to be governed by the coercive and punitive rule of law in order to avoid destroying themselves and one another: "the law brings wrath" (Rom. 4:15), legal authority being "the servant of God, an avenger who carries out wrath on the wrongdoer" (Rom. 13:4). The biblical admonition, "Vengeance is mine, I will repay, says the Lord" (Deut. 32:35; Rom. 12:19) refers, then, to the vengeance taken by both the angelic and human agents of God's wrath, the legal authorities who rule over an unbelieving world that exists independently of the biblical God's rule of love. Moreover, it refers to the day of judgment, which Jesus called the "end of the age" (Matt. 13:39-40, 49) because it would mean the necessary end of the kingdoms of the present age due to the arrival of the coming age of the kingdom of God (see Luke 18:29-30; 20:34-35).

II

That the biblical God does not experience resentment toward and alienation from his human creatures and, therefore, *does not need to forgive so as to be reconciled to them*, however, does not mean that human beings do not need forgiveness. The offender, once realizing his or her offense, naturally perceives the offended party as angry and hostile and, therefore, demanding payment, even when the offended party does not hold the offense against the offender. This is especially the case when the offended party is absent, and the offender can only guess how the offended party may feel. In that God is absent to the physical senses, his human creatures can only perceive him according to whatever the word "God" may, both consciously and unconsciously, mean to them. And all three of the monotheistic religions – Judaism, Christianity and Islam – have historically reinforced the perception of an alienated God by projecting an anthropomorphic image of an angry deity who must be appeased before he can show favor.

This is the biblical paradox created by the Mosaic law, which comprised the legal debt against the people of God, defining them as transgressors and, therefore, as (metaphorically speaking) debtors needing forgiveness. As long as the Mosaic law stood as the ruling authority over God's people, it would stand between them and God, pronouncing them guilty, blocking their entrance into God's favor. And in so doing, the Mosaic law would block the access of all, namely Gentiles, who would seek God.

Despite the many Mosaic and prophetic testimonies regarding God's lovingkindness (Hebrew, *chesed*) toward his people, the old covenant could not help but project an image, and therefore instill in Israel the perception, of an angry God. As "letter," the Mosaic law, despite its testimony to the righteousness of its God of promise, could only condemn God's old-covenant people not only because of their transgressions, but also because it could not soften their hearts so as to open their hearts to God's loving word of promise.

The forgiveness needed by all who would seek God was the end of the old covenant "letter," which was the legal debt of sin that stood between God and his people.

God, then, paid the legal debt of sin through the agency of Jesus' crucifixion, not because he demanded, or needed, payment in order to forgive sins but because all who would be God's people needed to be persuaded that God was wholly and fully for them and, therefore, would not hold their sins against them when they came to him through faith in his promise. Further, they needed to be persuaded that the coming day of judgment would be, for them, the day of salvation rather than the day of destruction.

God's payment of the debt of sin, then, neither enabled nor nullified his forgiveness of the debt. God's forgiveness/cancellation of the unpaid debt is the *figurative expression* of God's termination of the rule of the Mosaic law. God needed no payment in order to love all, and to accept all who would come to him through faith in his promise. Nor did God need to terminate the Mosaic law in order to relate to believers as his children. Instead, the need for forgiveness exists in the hearts of those who would believe God's promise. The Mosaic law would demand payment as long as it remained in effect as the agent of God's rule over his people. As such, its demand for payment would continue to stand between God and his people, preventing them from opening their hearts to God's love.

In order to provide "the knowledge of sin" to God's people, the Mosaic law intensified the alienating effect of sin – "in order that sin might be shown to be sin, and through the commandment might become sinful beyond measure" (Rom. 7:13) – creating an image of the biblical God even more frightening, and thus alienating, than the images of the capricious and vindictive gods of the nations.

Therefore, to persuade all who would be his new-covenant people, both Jew and Gentile, that the time of the condemning old-covenant rule of the Mosaic law had come to an end – and the time of the justifying new-covenant rule of his Messiah had arrived – God paid the debt himself, as it were, *via* the agency of Jesus' crucifixion. God paid the debt not because he needed payment in order to cancel it but so that all who would seek the biblical God could believe with assurance that no debt of sin stood between them and their God.

The atonement of God's Messiah, Jesus, was not a *legal transaction*, therefore, carried out between and among the so-called "Persons of the Godhead," in order to allow them, one and all, to justify the extension and distribution of "the forgiveness of sins" to sinners. Instead, the atonement of Jesus was, and is, a *rhetorical interaction* – an act of persuasion – between God and his people, and all who would be his people from among all nations. The atonement is God's power to persuade all who would come to him through the faith of Jesus that they are "not under law but under grace" (Rom. 6:14); to persuade them that "There is therefore now no condemnation for those who are in Christ Jesus" (Rom. 8:1), so that they can now "draw near with a true heart in full assurance of faith" (Heb. 10:22).

And so, *forgiveness*, like *propitiation* and *redemption*, is a powerful metaphor signifying the termination of the Mosaic law and, by extension, the end of all accusing and condemning religious laws that would stand between the biblical God and all who would seek him.

III

God simply loves and, therefore, accepts all who come to him in faith: "And without faith it is impossible to please him, for whoever would draw near to God must believe that he exists and that he rewards those who seek him" (Heb. 11:6). There has never been a barrier in the heart of the biblical God to the entrance of his human creatures into his favor. As far as the biblical writers are concerned, the barrier has always, since the alienation of humanity from God in "Adam," been the unbelief in human hearts, manifested in the worship of other gods, not only ancient and religious but modern and secular as well. The prerequisite to coming to the biblical God in faith is turning away from whatever other gods one worships. This is biblical "repentance" (Greek, *metanoia*, literally, "change of mind"), and results in the change of behavior, from self-serving to other-serving, that Paul called "faith working through love" (Gal. 5:6).

All believers – other than those pseudo-believers who have, in their own eyes, succeeded in justifying themselves through their obedience to some religious law – recognize the threat that doubt of salvation and fear of punishment pose to their faith. The experience of "a true heart in full assurance of faith" (Heb. 10:22) is the experience of *being fully persuaded of the love of God*, which "casts out fear [f]or fear has to do with punishment, and whoever fears has not been perfected in love" (1 John 4:18).

Which is to say that God's love cannot be merely a matter of assent, leaving the inner person unchanged. The love of God must penetrate and permeate human consciousness – "the renewal of your mind" (Rom. 12:2), "to be renewed in the spirit of your mind" (Eph. 4:23) – in order to transform lives from the inside out. This is not a religious experience, the work of a mystical revelation experienced by a chosen few. The experience of God's love is, for the NT writers, the work of the NT message itself: the rhetorical experience of being understandingly persuaded by "the word of the cross" (1 Cor. 1:18). (A work that the evangelical gospel, with its legalistic God, is hard-pressed to do, leaving Christians forever in need of pre-fabricated religious experiences to assure them of God's love.) When Paul wrote that "God's love has been poured into our hearts through the Holy Spirit" (Rom. 5:5), he referred not to a religious experience beyond words but to a rhetorical experience of the word of God: the experience of being persuaded by the NT message of the demonstration of God's love in the atonement of Jesus.

The blood of Jesus did and does nothing to effect a change in God's attitude or disposition toward human beings; instead, "God shows his love for us in that while we were still sinners, Christ died for us" (Rom. 5:8). Paul's use of the present tense – "God shows his love for us" – means that God expresses, demonstrates, manifests his love for one and all whenever the NT message is heard. Which is to say that, for the NT writers, Jesus' crucifixion was, and continues to be, primarily a rhetorical act: *an act of persuasive power*.

Nothing took place *behind the scenes* during or after Jesus' crucifixion. God did not *literally* turn his back on his Son, though Jesus' echoing of

Psalm 22:1 – "My God, my God, why have you forsaken me?" (Mark 15:34) – was the sincere expression of how Jesus must have felt. Nor did the crucified and risen Jesus *literally* approach the judgment seat of God with the offering of his blood, turning God's wrath away from sinners and procuring his favor. This is a metaphorical image with a rhetorical intent: the intent is to persuade believers that they are not transgressors before an angry God but God's beloved "sons" (whether male or female) in identification with the Son. The only event that literally occurred was the crucifixion of Jesus itself, publically and graphically displayed for all to see.

And in light of Jesus' resurrection, "the word of the cross" became God's power to persuade the hearts of all who would hear and believe the NT message that the duration of the Mosaic law, and its condemnation of transgressors, had come to an end. That the old covenant, which had been written "on tablets of stone," had given way to a new covenant, written "on tablets of human hearts" (2 Cor. 3:3). That the heart-hardening coercion of "the letter" had been replaced by the heart-opening persuasion of "the spirit" (Rom. 7:6; 2 Cor. 3:6). That the day of judgment would be – rather than the day of destruction – the day of salvation for "everyone who calls on the name of the Lord" (Joel 2:32; Acts 2:21; Rom. 10:13).

Jesus' death on the cross, then, is God's persuasive power to deconstruct and dissolve the only barrier that has ever existed between God and his human creation: hardness of heart, which was necessarily elucidated and unavoidably intensified by the Mosaic law. And having served its necessary purpose and done its unavoidable damage, the rule of the Mosaic law was terminated at the cross.

IV

The paradox of God's freely-given – that is, unpaid-for – forgiveness *and* Jesus' payment of the legal debt must be recognized and accommodated by any theory of the atonement that would do justice (that is, be faithful) to the NT revelation of God in Christ. The most flagrant and fatal flaw of the evangelical rhetoric of the cross is that it fails at precisely this point.

That the NT idea of forgiveness is the cancellation of an *unpaid* debt is illustrated in Jesus' parable of the unforgiving servant (Matt. 18:21-35). The servant could not pay his financial debt to his master, who out of pity "released him and forgave him the debt" (Matt. 18:27). Neither the servant nor anyone else on the servant's behalf paid the debt. If anyone else had paid the servant's debt, Jesus could not have rightfully said that the master "forgave him the debt." The servant subsequently had a fellow servant, who owed but couldn't pay him a much smaller debt, thrown into debtors' prison. When his master heard of this, he said, "I forgave you all that debt because you pleaded with me. And should you not have had mercy on your fellow servant, as I had mercy on you?" And so he imprisoned his "wicked servant" (Matt. 18:32-33). This judgment upon the unforgiving servant is the metaphorical representation of what "my heavenly Father will do to every one of you, if you do not forgive your brother from your heart" (Mat. 18:35). Which is to say that the flip side of opening one's heart to God's forgiveness and becoming its instrument in the lives of others is to harden one's heart to it and perpetuate one's alienation from the God who offers it to one and all.

The meaning of the parable, then, emerges as Jesus converts the literal, or economic, meaning of forgiveness in the parable to the figurative, or spiritual, meaning for his followers, who must "forgive your brother from your heart." The God and Father of Jesus, then, is one who freely forgives, expecting only that the forgiven forgive others as freely ("from your heart") as they have been forgiven: "You received without paying; give without pay" (Matt. 10:8).

God's forgiveness of sins and his people's forgiveness of one another and others is, of course, qualitatively different. The *literal/financial* meaning of forgiveness applies to God's forgiveness of sins in the sense of his canceling the *figurative/legal* debt of the Mosaic law. This same *literal/financial* meaning of forgiveness applies to believers' forgiveness of others in the sense of their canceling the *figurative/moral* debt they imagine they are owed by those who wrong them. In the biblical God's reality, believers are not owed a *moral* debt by those who offend them, any more than God considers that he is owed a *moral* debt by sinners. The difference, however, is that "God is love" while believers still struggle with the human tendency to hold offenses against the offender, issuing *moral* debts and demanding payment. Nevertheless, followers of Jesus are called to forgive – to cancel the imagined, unpaid moral debts of their offenders – as freely as God cancelled their metaphorical, unpaid legal debt through the atonement of their Messiah.

When *forgiveness* lost its primary literal connection with the world of finance, its *figurative/moral* application to human relationships began to seem like its literal and only meaning. And, as a result, the critical feature of forgiveness as the cancellation of an *unpaid* debt was lost. Somehow the idea emerged that forgiveness could depend on some form of payment, some kind of restitution, as an effort to "make up for it." Perhaps this rhetorical reinvention of forgiveness related more or less directly to the third-century emphasis on the necessity of "penance" for acceptance into the emerging institutional "Church" (see Chapter 1). Whatever the case, once forgiveness lost its primary economic sense, it seems no longer to have necessarily excluded the idea of payment from its meaning.

The evangelical failure to apply *in a figurative way* the literal, economic meaning of forgiveness – as cancellation of an unpaid debt – to its doctrine of the atonement has resulted in a distorted and misshapen image of the biblical God. The picture (reinforced by the literalization of God's "wrath") is of a God who is angry with sinners and whose forgiveness – understood as his change of attitude toward sinners, from negative to positive – is contingent upon, first, *payment exacted from his Son* (who, in Trinitarian terms, is part of *Godself*) and, second, *penance enacted by sinners*. Which is to say that God does not forgive (and, therefore, remains unforgiving) unless both prerequisites are satisfied. The satisfaction of these prerequisites is necessary, according to the evangelical doctrine, due to God's "justice" (understood in a *legal* rather than the *covenantal* sense elaborated in Chapter 1).

The evangelical idea that God could somehow be both *loving*, in terms of his intent to sacrifice his Son for sinners, *and* yet *unforgiving* toward sinners apart from the effect of that sacrifice can only result in an image of a schizophrenic deity. *For it is impossible to be both loving and unforgiving at the same time.* In fact, the human act of forgiveness – in the moral rather than the economic sense – is necessary only because human love cannot approximate the love of God, so that the more grievously human beings are wronged, the harder it is for them not to hold those wrongs against the wrong-doers. And the more their sense of justice demands that the wrong-doers pay! And the more difficult it is for them to forgive.

But God's holiness, far from being an intolerance of imperfection, expresses itself in that God, unlike human beings, does not himself demand payment for wrongs but, instead, seeks to persuade wrong-doers – at such cost to himself – that nothing stands between them and him but their own unwillingness to be reconciled.

The cognitive dissonance created by the *theological dichotomy* of a God who loves but cannot forgive without payment virtually ensures that the evangelical rhetoric of the cross will sabotage the experience of a "true heart with full assurance of faith" (Heb. 10:22) that a NT understanding of the atonement of Jesus is intended to instill within believers of the NT message.

V

The outstanding NT illustration of how alien the God of the evangelical rhetoric of the cross is to the God and Father of Jesus is Jesus' parable of the lost, or prodigal, son (see Luke 15:11-32).

The son recklessly squanders his share of his inheritance until he is penniless and homeless, returns to his father anticipating that he will have to work out a payment for whatever favor his father may show him, and is surprised to find his father welcoming him with open arms and throwing a feast in his honor: "And bring the fattened calf and kill it, and let us eat and celebrate. For this son was dead, and is alive again; he was lost, and is found" (Luke 15:23-24).

In this case, "the fattened calf" is sacrificed not to pay off any debt – least of all as a payment the father makes to himself to justify forgiving his son – but *to persuade the son of his father's forgiveness*. And the story gives no indication that the father – unlike his older son – nurses any feelings of resentment or hostility that the father must give up in order to forgive his lost-and-found son. The forgiveness itself, then, just as the sacrifice of the fattened calf, is purely for the benefit of his son. That is, to provide the son with assurance that his father's love is unconditional, that his acceptance is genuine and authentic. To banish the inevitable doubt and fear in the heart of the son regarding his standing with his father, so that the reconciliation of son and father will be complete.

As far as the story is concerned, the father himself has never been alienated from his son, has never held against him his son's immature foolishness or wanton defiance, and, to the contrary, is waiting with open arms upon his son's return.

This is the image of God that the NT Jesus projected and reflected with both his words and his deeds. And this is the image of God that the biblical message conveys to a world of potential believers. An image that has been subverted and perverted by the evangelical rhetoric of the cross.

The parable of the lost son gives a far truer account of the meaning of the atonement than does all of the convoluted theological gymnastics of the evangelical doctrine of the atonement. The Lord's Supper (see Matt. 26:26-29; Mark 14:22-25; Luke 22:14-23; 1 Cor. 11:23-26), during which believers symbolically eat the flesh and drink the blood of God's Anointed, is precisely analogous to the feast thrown by the father for his lost-and-found son. The Lord's Supper clearly anticipates the eschatological feast at the coming of the kingdom of God: "I tell you, many will come from east and west and recline at table with Abraham, Isaac, and Jacob in the kingdom of heaven" (Matt. 8:11); "I tell you I will not drink again of this fruit of the vine until the day when I drink it new with you in my Father's kingdom" (Matt. 26:29); "For as often as you eat this bread and drink this cup, you proclaim the Lord's death until he comes" (1 Cor. 11:26).

In fact, feasting on Jesus' flesh and blood is a NT metaphor for faith in the NT message: "Whoever feeds on my flesh and drinks my blood has eternal life [literally, 'life in the coming age'], and I will raise him up on the last day" (John 6:54). The purpose of this feasting on the flesh and blood that Jesus sacrificed on the cross – whether symbolically during the Lord's Supper or metaphorically in the life of faith – is precisely the purpose of the feast thrown by the father for the lost-and-found son: *to fully persuade believers of their acceptance by the God and Father of Jesus, and therefore, of the assurance of their salvation through resurrection at the end of the present age.*

Forgiveness of sins is, therefore, a NT metaphor – the cancellation of an unpaid debt – intended to persuade with assurance all who seek the biblical God that the rule of the Mosaic law has ended, that God will not hold their sins against them on the day of judgment, that they are as fully acceptable to God, as righteous in God's eyes, as Jesus himself. In short, that the One they seek welcomes them with unconditional love.

> "For God did not send his Son into the world to condemn the world, but in order that the world might be saved through him" (John 3:17).

Endnotes

i.   *Theological Dictionary of the New Testament*, ed. Gerhard Kittel and Gerhard Friedrich, trans. Geoffrey W. Bromiley. Grand Rapids: William B. Eerdmans Publishing Company, 1985, p. 229.

EPILOGUE

The Rhetorical Question

So what? What difference does the foregoing understanding of the crucifixion of Jesus make?

The primary argument of this book is that the intended effect of the crucifixion of Jesus as far as the NT writers were concerned, was not *legal* but *rhetorical*. Primary argument of this book.

To say that its NT purpose was *not legal* is to say, contrary to the evangelical rhetoric of the cross, that Jesus' crucifixion did not satisfy the misconceived demand of God's legal justice for satisfaction in the form of the innocent blood of his Son. (To be clear, any theory of the atonement is *rhetorical*, in that it amounts to an argument for a certain interpretation of the NT data. The evangelical rhetoric of the cross, however, presents itself as *the* NT doctrine of the atonement, rather than as a matter of interpretation – subject to persuasive discourse among interpreters – and therefore conceals its *rhetorical* character.)

To say that the NT purpose of Jesus' crucifixion was *rhetorical* rather than *legal* is to say that its power was – and, if so, continues to be – entirely persuasive. It is to say that the crucifixion of Jesus was not required by a legal demand, located somewhere in the heart of God, for payment as a legal justification for the forgiveness of sins. In Paul's words, "in Christ, God was reconciling the world to himself, not counting their trespasses against them, and entrusting to us the message of reconciliation. Therefore, we are ambassadors for Christ, God making his appeal through us. We implore you on behalf of Christ, be reconciled to God" (2 Cor. 5:19-20). For Paul, God's work "in Christ" of "reconciling the world to himself" *was the same thing as* God's "appeal." That is to say, Jesus' crucifixion did not automatically effect reconciliation between "the world" and the biblical God. Rather, Jesus' crucifixion (in light of his resurrection) was God's "appeal," issuing forth through the NT message that Paul and his apostolic associates proclaimed. The terms "appeal" and "implore" indicate the rhetorical, which is to say, the persuasive, character of not only Paul's work as messenger but of the content of his message.

The persuasive "appeal" of "the word of the cross" (1 Cor. 1:18) was intended to radically reorient its hearers' understanding of God and, as a result, of how to relate not only to God but to themselves as well.

I

For Paul, the Mosaic law constituted a "veil" (2 Cor. 3:13-16) over the hearts of the Israelites, preventing them from seeing the true face of God. Paul drew his veil-metaphor from the story about Moses' reception of the law from *Yahweh* (see Exo. 34:29-35). According to the story, Moses' face temporarily glows in reflected glory after receiving the law from *Yahweh*, and Moses veils his face, according to Paul, "so that the Israelites might not gaze at the outcome of what was being brought to an end" (2 Cor. 3:13). That is to say, the veiling of Moses' face led the Israelites to believe that the glory of the law of commandments was equal to the glory of *Yahweh* himself. And this resulted in the misconception that the rule of the law was identical to – and would be as everlasting as – the rule of God. This was, perhaps, intended – along with the terrifying pyrotechnics that surrounded the giving of the law at Mount Sinai (see Exo. 19:16-25) – to induce the Israelites to make a clean break with the gods of Egypt and to fully embrace *Yahweh* as their national god to the exclusion of other gods (which, as it turned out, took centuries). The eventual exclusive worship of *Yahweh* would be essential to prepare Israel for what would eventually be, according to the NT writers, the complete – as opposed to the partial – revelation of God in the coming of the Messiah.

The rule of the Mosaic law of commandments, in Paul's view, had been, from its inception, necessarily temporary, intended for eventual displacement by the Messianic law of love. Nevertheless, the ongoing misconception that the rule of the Mosaic law would be everlasting kept the majority of Paul's countrymen under its condemnation: "For to this day, when they read the old covenant, that same veil remains unlifted, because only through Christ is it taken away" (2 Cor. 3:14). The literal "veil" with which Moses covered his face to keep the Israelites from seeing the temporary character of the old-covenant law had become a figurative veil "over their hearts" (2 Cor. 3:15), keeping the majority of the Jews of Paul's day from seeing "the light of the gospel of the glory of Christ, who is the image of God" (2 Cor. 4:4).

Paul did *not* write that his countrymen were unable to "see" the later Trinitarian construct of Christ as God-in-human-form. Paul's subject was not *incarnation* (a term born of Greek philosophy, alien to the NT writers) but *covenant.* Most of Paul's Jewish contemporaries were unable to see that God had replaced the national covenant of the death-dealing "letter" with an international covenant of life-giving "spirit" (2 Cor. 3:6). They were unable to see that their God of law was a god of their own creation, that the new-covenant message had "shone in our hearts to give the light of the knowledge of the glory of God in the face of Jesus Christ" (2 Cor. 4:6). Which is to say that the truth about God's purpose, which had been obscured by the "veil" of the old-covenant law, had been revealed with unprecedented clarity in the new-covenant message of Jesus.

The NT understanding of *Yahweh* as a partial revelation of the biblical God is consistent with a literary understanding of the OT *Yahweh.* That is to say, an understanding of *Yahweh* not as a transparent rendering of God (which is, in any case, surely beyond the capacity of words) but as a literary character. Ancient historiography (i.e., the writing of history) was a rhetorical exercise, its purpose being to dramatize – and, in so doing, to reveal the meaning of – historical events, putting the intended interpretation of those events in the mouths of historical figures (whose exact words, in most cases, could not have been known), in order to persuade readers to accept that interpretation. The OT writers' intent was to persuade their readers to interpret the historical events of their oral tradition in terms of the progressive fulfillment of God's promise to Abraham to make of him a great nation (Israel, which would, according to the NT writers, become the conduit through which God would complete the fulfillment of that promise by blessing all nations in Abraham's seed, that is, through the Messiah). This progressive fulfillment of the Abrahamic promise took the form of a series of interventions by *Yahweh,* who is the central character – as well as the object of worship – in the OT narrative.

The OT character called *Yahweh* was the God of Israel, whose perception of its God was mediated through the Mosaic law. Consequently, from the NT standpoint, *Yahweh* was a partial rather than a complete revelation of the NT Father.[1] The NT writers did not use the name *Yahweh* for the Father. The OT texts quoted by the NT writers were taken from the *Septuagint*, the Greek translation of the Hebrew scriptures, which observed the tradition (adopted by English versions of the Old Testament) of substituting the title "Lord" (Greek, *Kurios*) for the name *Yahweh*. (English versions render *Yahweh* as "LORD," in all capitals to distinguish it from the Hebrew words for *Lord*: *Adonai*, referring to the *Lord* God, and *adoni*, referring to a human *lord*, such as a king or high official; *adoni* is used in Psa. 110:1, the OT text the NT writers most often quoted, for the Messiah.)

Unlike the OT *Yahweh*, the NT Father appears as a literary character only in a few exceptional instances, in the form of "a voice from heaven" (Matt. 3:17) at Jesus' baptism and "a voice from the cloud" (Matt. 17:5) at Jesus' transfiguration, and in Stephen's vision of "the Son of Man standing at the right hand of God" (Acts 7:56). The Father was consistently represented by the NT writers via the agency of his Son, the NT Jesus. This is consistent with the NT writers' avowed persuasive intent of presenting Jesus as the full and final revelation of God, *not* as God himself but as "the image of God" (2 Cor. 4:4), the complete and ultimate – as opposed to, in the case of the Mosaic law, the partial and intermediate – reflection of God.

For Paul, then, the OT character *Yahweh* is the *veiled God*. Which is to say that the OT *Yahweh* could not reveal the fullness of God's love for his people and for all nations, a love that was obscured by the demonic usurpation of the Mosaic law, which brought wrath on the people of Israel, and through Israel on the nations. The OT *Yahweh* possessed a dark side, then, reflecting the demonic opposition to God's purpose constituted by Israel's deification of the law (see Chapter 3). This exaltation of the Mosaic law into an idol amounted to the rhetorical invention of the god of law.

The "righteousness" of Jesus' God and Father was, by comparison, revealed "apart from the law" (Rom. 3:21), the NT message revealing a God not of law but of promise. This God is revealed *in part* by the OT writers

---

[1]   Which is not to identify *Yahweh* with the *Demiurge* of the second-century Gnostic leader Marcion, and of Gnostic Christianity in general. The Gnostic *Demiurge* was the inferior "God" who created the world of evil in an effort to obscure the true knowledge of God. By comparison, the OT *Yahweh* was the God of Israel, which is to say, God as Israel perceived him: the revelation of God preserved in the Hebrew scriptures comes through the eyes of the prophets of Israel and the Israelite scribes who interpreted their message.

as the God of the Abrahamic promise but, as far as Paul was concerned, the OT *Yahweh* could not represent the fullness of God because of the angelic mediation of the Mosaic law and its demonic usurpation (see Chapter 2). For Paul, the fullness of God is revealed in Jesus, whose God and Father takes the life of humanity, condemned by law to abide in the darkness of guilt and fear and death, and fills it with the promise of hope.

While the foregoing is a necessarily nuanced interpretation of the biblical portrayal of God, the alternative is to take the biblical God *at face value*. Which is to say that the alternative is to view God as having two faces, one of love and mercy toward those who love him and the other of wrath and vengeance toward those who don't. This book has made a concerted effort to expose the latter face as the pseudo-justice of a pseudo-God.

II

The Bible, for evangelical Christianity, is "the word of God." Precisely what it means to identify the Bible as the word of God is a matter of some debate among evangelical scholars and leaders, divisions being created mostly by various theories of "inspiration" concerning "infallibility" and "inerrancy." Nevertheless, the unified view of evangelicalism is the identification of the words of the Bible with "the word of God."

What this equation between the Bible and the word of God has meant in the history of Christianity has been to make no clear distinction between promise and law in regard to the word of God. Which is to say that both the biblical God's Abrahamic promise and his Mosaic law (which came, according to Paul, 430 years after the promise) have been viewed equally – that is, in an undifferentiated sense – as the word of God. And the fact that the Mosaic law continues to be the evangelical word of God in the same sense as (and, in practice, in a far more prominent sense than) the Abrahamic promise and its fulfillment means that the commandments of the Mosaic law – or some reformulation of them as evangelical Christian law – continue to condemn those who attempt to worship the evangelical God.

Moreover, the ongoing identification of the Mosaic law with the word of God has given the entire Bible the appearance of a code of conduct, biblical instruction taking the primary form of commandments. And because the evangelical word of God governs believers, first and foremost, via commandments, the Mosaic law (as opposed to the Abrahamic promise) is evangelical Christianity's paradigm for understanding the Bible. In this sense, evangelical Christianity is the true heir of rabbinic Judaism, with which Paul took issue for subordinating the Abrahamic promise to the Mosaic law (see Chapter 2).

All of which is to say that, in popular (that is, evangelical) Christian understanding, the legal-justice paradigm governs the perception of the Bible as a book of law and of its God as a God of law.

This book has sought to replace the *Latin, legal-justice paradigm* that has ruled the tradition of Christianity from early in the post-apostolic period – and led to the rhetorical invention of the evangelical doctrine of the atonement – with the *Hebrew, covenantal-justice paradigm*. This covenantal-justice paradigm replaces law with promise as the form in which the biblical word of God presents itself. The word of God that was preserved by the biblical writers takes the form of a message of promise-and-fulfillment: of the promise to Abraham to make of him a great nation and to bless all nations in his seed, and of the progressive fulfillment of that promise. Accordingly, the OT writers told the story of God's fulfillment of the great-nation promise in the old-covenant history of Israel (in which the Mosaic law played an essential role), and the NT writers told the story of the fulfillment of the international-blessing promise in the new-covenant history of Jesus.

To hear the word of God's promise and its fulfillment *with understanding* required knowledge of the history of Israel from its ancient origins in Abraham to the first-century circumstances in which Jesus made his appearance, and the biblical writers told the story in narrative form as well as in other literary forms, both poetic and apocalyptic. The biblical storyline is the historical framework for hearing – that is to say, understanding – *the message of promise-and-fulfillment,* which is itself the biblical word of God.

That the OT writers understood this is evident from the fact that they typically introduced the word of *Yahweh* in their own writings with words like, "Thus says *Yahweh*," portraying *the word* as coming to a certain prophet, who subsequently delivers it to the people. That is to say, the narrative is not itself the word of God but *is about the revelation of the word of God*. The word of God, for the OT writers, was not a *written artifact* but a *spoken message*, which was subsequently embedded and preserved in oral traditions, from which the biblical writers drew to compose their narratives.

Likewise, the NT writers identified the word of God not with their writings but with what they called "the gospel" (see 1 Thes. 2:9, 13; 1 Pet. 1:23-25), the *spoken message* of Jesus which he entrusted to his apostles, who in turn proclaimed it to the nations. Even Paul, who was both speaker and writer, wrote his letters *about the spoken message* that his readers had previously heard from him or one of his apostolic associates. (See, for examples, 1 Cor. 2:1-5 and 1 Thes. 2:2.)

Rather than identifying the word of God with the Bible, then, truer to the biblical writers themselves is to distinguish their words from the word of God in the same sense as messengers are distinguished from their message. The Bible itself is the messenger, while the word of God is the biblical message. The Bible contains no "theory of inspiration." Whatever "inspiration" may mean with reference to the biblical writers themselves, they saw their work as the faithful preservation of the word of God – the message of the Messianic fulfillment of God's Abrahamic promise – for their own and whatever generations might follow. Whatever poetic license they took in constructing their historical narratives, their intent was to faithfully preserve the message, which they considered the word of God.

Nevertheless, contrary to the OT writers' understanding of the word of God in terms of the Abrahamic promise-and-fulfillment, the tradition of Pharisaic (what subsequently became rabbinic) Judaism had long exalted the Mosaic law as the paradigm for understanding the Hebrew scriptures. And it had constructed "the tradition of the elders" (Matt. 15:2; Mark 7:5) as a religious system of observances that would ostensibly ensure obedience to the commandments. This approach to the Hebrew scriptures and to faith itself set Jesus at odds with the Pharisees and Paul with the Judaizers (i.e., those Jewish believers who sought to impose the Jewish interpretation of the Mosaic law on Gentile believers).

Jesus was not a Biblicist. Like most Jews of his day, he was schooled in the Law and the Prophets and a student thereof, and his teaching drew liberally from them, rooting his own sense of mission and destiny in the Hebrew prophetic tradition. Nevertheless, the NT Jesus clearly saw himself as extending, and moving beyond, the limits of the Hebrew scriptures (or, at least, the limits that Pharisaic Judaism had placed on them).

Likewise, the Pauline dichotomy of "spirit" (literally, *breath*) and "letter" makes clear that Paul did not view his own writings – and if not his, certainly not those of his apostolic colleagues – as a new holy book intended to establish and govern a new religious faith. For Paul, the Mosaic law and its scriptures – understood and observed by first-century Jews as a holy book of religious authority – had been misconstrued and, consequently, turned into a death-dealing "letter" (2 Cor. 3:6), to which followers of Jesus "have died" (Rom. 7:4). The "letter" had, therefore, given way to the life-giving "breath" of the NT message. And the intent of Paul's letters was not to codify that message into a religious system but simply to explain its implications for and applications to a first-century life of freedom and responsibility: freedom from religious authority, on one hand, and responsibility to exercise freedom lovingly, on the other: "For freedom Christ has set us free; stand firm therefore, and do not submit again to a yoke of slavery" (Gal. 5:1); "For you were called to freedom, brothers. Only do not use your freedom as an opportunity for the flesh, but through love serve one another" (Gal. 5:13).

All of which is to say that the apostolic understanding of the crucifixion of Jesus as the termination of the governing authority of the Mosaic law made a radical difference in the NT writers' approach to scripture. It could not, for them, take the form of legislation, of a code of conduct, of a list of commandments to be obeyed or disobeyed. Instead, the NT writers viewed both the Hebrew scriptures and their own writings as "able to make you wise for salvation through faith in Christ Jesus" and further conveying wisdom for "teaching, for reproof, for correction, and for training in righteousness" (2 Tim. 3:15-16).

While commandments do not necessarily preclude wisdom, neither do they require wisdom to be obeyed because they require no understanding other than that disobedience results in punishment. The NT writers, by comparison, emphasized the necessity of "wisdom and understanding" (Col. 1:9) as the NT alternative to law-keeping for followers of Jesus (see also Eph. 5:15-17; Jas. 1:5)

III

The argument that the crucifixion of Jesus, in light of his resurrection from the dead, was a rhetorical act of the biblical God – intended to persuade both Israel and the nations that the Mosaic law and its condemnation no longer stood between them and God – is complemented by the historical fact that Jesus' crucifixion was also a rhetorical act on the part of both the Jewish religious and Roman political establishments. (It was also a legal act in the sense that Jesus was crucified as both a religious and civil law-breaker, but this corresponded to no legal sentiment in the heart of the biblical God.) The joint action of (the Jewish) Church and (the Roman) State in collaborating to put Jesus to death was intended to persuade the Jewish people that for one to either remain or become a follower of Jesus of Nazareth was to become both a religious and a civil *outlaw*. The persuasive appeal, both verbally and visually, of the crucifixion of Jesus was that his followers would find nowhere to belong in the Church and State of their day.

From the NT point of view, however, the message of Jesus' crucifixion, in light of the apostolic witness to his subsequent resurrection, was that the very act whereby the ruling powers of Church and State had intended to silence Jesus once and for all had, to the contrary, announced the judgment of God on all religious and civil authority and power. Jesus' followers were now *free to be outlaws*, that is, to live outside the religious and civil laws that governed the nations, "for the one who loves has fulfilled the law" (Rom. 13:8) and, thus, no longer needs it.[2]

Admittedly, from all the indications left by the NT writers, the new-covenant community had to grow into that understanding of a law-free lifestyle. The chief controversy within that first-century community was the ongoing role of the Mosaic law of commandments. Was it to continue to govern the lives of God's covenant people, collapsing the new covenant into the old and making the Jesus-community a sect within the international Jewish community? Or was the Mosaic law to serve, as Paul insisted, as prophetic "witness" (Rom. 3:21) to the preparation of Israel for the coming of its Messiah, who had now replaced the Mosaic law of *letter* with the Messianic law of *spirit*? Paul heard, evidently sooner and more clearly than his apostolic colleagues, the call to the law-free lifestyle implicit in the Jesus-message and insisted that it be heeded.

That Paul ultimately failed in his efforts is evident from the subsequent history of "Christianity" as it has unfolded to the present day. Evidence of Paul's failure to establish a law-free ethic as the norm for the emerging Christian tradition is found in NT sayings whose plain import remains alien to the teaching and practice of Christianity.

---

[2] The only "law" approved by the NT writers was the unwritten law of love embodied by Jesus, whose servanthood and sacrifice constructed the model of life for his followers. The NT "law of Christ" (Gal. 6:2) was a model of "faith working through love" (Gal. 5:6), which is to say that followers of Jesus loved as they understood that they had been loved by God through the servanthood and sacrifice of his Messiah. To live this way would, of course, preclude any arbitrary violation of civil law (see Rom. 13; 1 Pet. 2:13-17), but it would also promote any violation of civil law that the well-being of another made necessary (see Acts 5:29). The complexity of life and the frequently gray area between right and wrong necessitated the emphasis on wisdom as the NT alternative to law-keeping (see, for examples, Eph. 5:15-17; Col. 1:9-10; Jas. 1:5)

> "But you are not to be called rabbi, for you have one teacher and
> you are all brothers" (Matt. 23:8).

The NT Jesus' words do not prohibit his followers from teaching one another, an informal activity in which the older and more experienced – those the NT writers called "elders" – would naturally engage in relation to the younger. What Jesus' words clearly oppose is the elevation of some of his followers over others by means of religious titles signifying religious positions of authority. Rabbis were the teachers of the Jewish law, and their words possessed a religious authority that presumed to mediate either God's acceptance or God's rejection. This is precisely the effect of the words of those teachers of the Christian law who are called "Minister" and "Pastor" and "Preacher" and "Priest" and "Bishop" (not to mention, "Pope"), among other religious titles assigned by Protestantism and Catholicism and other forms of organized Christianity. The authority of these official positions, while not always spelled out in Church law, is nevertheless implicit in the titles themselves, allowing those Church leaders who so wish, to "lord it over," which is to say, to "exercise authority over" Church members (Matt. 20:25). Of course, the gradual post-apostolic reordering of the community of Jesus-followers from an *informal association* into a *religious organization* necessitated that leadership – which had previously taken the Hebrew form of example and persuasion – become lordship according to the Greco-Roman model: "the rulers of the Gentiles lord it over them, and their great ones exercise authority over them" (Matt. 20:25).

> "Love does no wrong to a neighbor; therefore love is the fulfilling
> of the law" (Rom. 13:10).

This is evidently Paul's interpretation of the great-commandment saying of Jesus: "On these two commandments [enjoining love for God and for neighbor as for self] depend all the Law and the Prophets" (Matt. 22:40). Paul takes Jesus' meaning to be that love – understood as the doing of good toward one and all – fulfills the law by going beyond its negative requirements: "You shall not murder"; "You shall not commit adultery"; "You shall not steal"; etc. The question, then, for Jesus-followers is not, "What is the requirement of the law?" – whether of the Mosaic law or of some reformulated Christian spin-off thereof – but "What is the requirement of love?" And unlike the commandments of law, the answer to the love-question always depends on the situation. The question amounts to how, in every situation, to love as God has shown his love in the biblical message about Jesus (see Eph. 4:32-5:2; Col.

3:12-13; 1 John 3:16-18). To answer this question requires wisdom rather than commandments.[3]

> "'All things are lawful for me,' but not all things are helpful. All
> things are lawful for me,' but I will not be enslaved by anything.'"
> (1 Cor. 6:12).

> "'All things are lawful,' but not all things are helpful. 'All things
> are lawful,' but not all things build up" (1 Cor. 10:23).

The words, "All things are lawful for me" (6:12) and "All things are lawful" (10:23) appear in quotation marks in English versions (though quotation marks do not appear in the original language) because of the scholarly consensus that Paul was quoting a faction in the Corinthian community of faith which had interpreted Paul's teaching of salvation by grace apart from works to mean that they were free to behave as they wished, without regard for consequences. While this seems likely, Paul did not contradict their claim regarding the lawfulness of any behavior in which they wished to engage. After all, if the biblical God had terminated his biblical law, then any desired behavior might be justified by the now-familiar refrain: "There's no law against it." Instead of objecting that certain kinds of behavior indeed did violate God's law, however, Paul reinterpreted their words in terms of love. Which is to say that when choices must be made, the question is not whether or not a particular behavior is "lawful" but whether or not it is "helpful" (Greek, *symphero*), also rendered "profitable" or "expedient."

Expedience is a function of value in the sense that the expedient act facilitates the acquisition or achievement of whatever is valued, whatever is considered profitable. In terms of conventional values, this means what is economically or politically profitable, the respective values being money or power, respectively. When considered in economic and/or political terms, then, expedience seems to regard the rightness or wrongness of any action

---

[3] The by-now-all-too-familiar question, "What would Jesus do?" may appear to be an alternative to law-keeping, but it may, in practice, serve as a motivational reinforcement to law-keeping. The answer may be that Jesus would surely obey the relevant commandment, as opposed to an answer that would require drawing wisdom from an understanding of the biblical message. This understanding is what Paul prayed for his readers.

is irrelevant. For Paul, however, the sole value by which all decision-making and subsequent behavior was measured is love. Love becomes the standard by which the rightness or wrongness of all actions is measured.

As far as Paul was concerned, love requires, first, the freedom to choose, for actions that are either coerced by law or compelled by desire are incompatible with love, which can neither be coerced or compelled but can only be freely expressed. And, second, love requires equating the interests of others with one's own, which is to say that to act for oneself at another's expense is incompatible with love. Therefore, what is expedient for Paul has nothing to do with money or power; instead, the expedient act is the one that expedites one's own freedom from external coercion or internal compulsion, and that accrues to the benefit of those in one's sphere of influence.

Consequently, the first consideration for whether an action is "helpful" is whether it serves individual freedom: "'All things are lawful for me,' but I will not be enslaved by anything" (1 Cor. 6:12). Human appetites – Paul's immediate concern being the male appetite for sex, and whether or not to gratify it with the aid of temple prostitutes, as was the common practice of Corinthian males – can easily become addictions, which rob human beings of their freedom. Contrary to the post-apostolic theologians (most notably Augustine) who demonized sexual desire and equated sexual intercourse with the "original sin," Paul warned only against the deification of sexual desire because, like all forms of idolatry, it was antithetical to individual freedom. To become a slave to desire, whether sexual or chemical or other, is to forfeit human agency, the freedom to make choices. *No, contrary to (God's Command)*

The second consideration is whether an action serves the community: "'All things are lawful,' but not all things build up [or *edify*]. Let no one seek his own good [literally, *the thing of oneself*], but the good of his neighbor [literally, *the thing of the other*]." Paul was not here admonishing against self-interest as such but against the human tendency to pursue self-interest without regard for the interests of others, which so often means at the expense of others.

To love one's neighbor as oneself is to pursue a natural self-interest with an equal concern for the interests of others. This, of course, requires a wisdom that goes far beyond that required by law-keeping.

The history of Christian law-keeping is the history not only of the suppression of individual freedom by religious authority but also of the invention of loopholes in every variety of Christian law to allow some Christians – especially the clergy – to be more equal than others in regard to the pursuit of self-interest.

To be an *outlaw* in the Jesus-tradition, then, is to reject not only the coercion of law but also the compulsion of desire. Which is to say that living outside the law requires *not* the demonization of desire, whether for sexual pleasure or material fortune, but the subjection of desire to the priority of love (which is served by some desires and betrayed by others).

Desire is a raw fact of human life, and the biblical writers neither demonized nor deified it. Instead, they advocated the satisfaction of some desires and the suppression of others, in the interest of one's own freedom and the well-being of others. While the NT writers advocated the *suppression* of desires that would lead to self-destructive or anti-social behavior, they never advocated the *repression* of any desire, that is, the denial that one is experiencing a given desire. Repression of desire is another negative effect of the legal orientation of evangelical Christianity, which often confuses *resisting* the desire – that is, the temptation – to do wrong with *eliminating* the desire to do wrong, as if this were a function of spiritual growth. The legally perfect human being, of course, would be one who had no desire to break the law. Even the NT Jesus, however, desired to do wrong in that he "in every respect has been tempted as we are" (Heb. 4:15), one being "tempted when he is lured and enticed by his own desire" (Jas. 1:14). The NT claim that Jesus was "without sin" (Heb. 4:15) means *not* that he was without the desires that are common to all human beings but that he alternatively satisfied or suppressed his desires according to the priority of love. And to love is to practice the *covenantal justice* of faithfulness to God and to others.

IV

The difference, then, that the crucifixion of Jesus was intended by the NT writers to make was to radically alter the orientation of faith toward God. Faith has, throughout religious history, had a legal orientation toward God (or gods).[4] And this legal orientation has colored faith with guilt and fear, which are the only motivational tools available to gods of law. The evangelical doctrine of the atonement creates a loophole in the divine legal system, created

---

4   Even Eastern religious faith promotes a form of legalism in the doctrine of
      karma: the moral law of cause and effect. One is deserving of whatever good
      or ill fortune befalls one due to actions not only of one's present life but also
      of one's past lives.

by the crucifixion of Jesus, which allows its law-God to suspend punishment and assume the role of loving Father – albeit not very persuasively – while yet remaining the law-God, who must, therefore, uphold the divine legal system. Even as he is ostensibly called "Father," then, he remains the law-God whose sense of divine-legal justice required that he demand the payment of innocent blood as the price of forgiveness. How can such a God motivate his worshipers with hope and love rather than with guilt and fear?

Evangelical Christianity will continue to worship law-God – animated and energized by its rhetoric of the cross – because it needs guilt and fear to reinforce its hold on its adherents. As do virtually all forms of organized religion.

The religion of the biblical God was organized in the form of the OT Church-State of Israel. A law of commandments was necessary to inspire guilt and fear in the Israelites because their Egyptian-Canaanite orientation toward the *category of being* known as "gods" did not include the possibility of a mutual loving faithfulness between worshipers and their gods. Loving faithfulness to *Yahweh* was, according to the OT writers, always the exception to the rule in old-covenant Israel.

But then the biblical God did something entirely unexpected. He shut down his own religion. And in so doing, he abrogated the necessity of religion altogether.

Religion can be defined, from an evolutionary standpoint, as "a system of emotionally binding beliefs and practices in which a society implicitly negotiates through prayer and sacrifice with supernatural agents, securing from them commands that compel members, through fear of divine punishment, to subordinate their interests to the common good."[i] From this point of view, religion is better understood as primarily a social, and only secondarily as a personal, phenomenon due to its demonstrated historical character of shaping social behavior. Both within and between societies, religion established moral standards long before the rise of legal agencies and institutions in ancient cultures: "Without a police force or prison guards or judiciary, in any case impossible for hunter gatherers, early societies achieved through religion both social cohesion and effective compliance with the dictates of an invisible government."[ii]

The scientific argument that religion may be an evolved part of human nature conflicts with faith in the biblical God only to the extent that religion itself is believed to be organically related to God. That is to say, that religion is, in some sense, a God-given vehicle for connecting, or reconnecting, with God, necessary because God's existence and presence are not directly evident or accessible to human perception. This is, of course, the assumption that underlies all religious faith: that religion – whether formally organized or in the relatively unorganized form called "spirituality" – is the means by which human beings relate to "God." (It then befalls the religious truth seeker to determine which among the variety of religious traditions is the most correct in its approach.)

If, however, the biblical God is *not* organically related to *religion* of any kind – whether Jewish, Christian or other – then the idea that religion is a product of human evolution does not necessarily threaten biblical faith (at least as it is portrayed on these pages). And the idea that the biblical God would use religion – in the form of the Mosaic law – for a temporary period and purpose, by way of transition from human immaturity to maturity, becomes far less incomprehensible.

Gal. 4:1–11

Evolution is primarily concerned with what features, not only biological but also social, contribute to the preservation of species: "Natural selection, a motive force of evolution, is about survival and who leaves more children."[iii] Religious faith, then, may have been selected in the process of human evolution (in the uncontroversial sense of natural selection) because it served two purposes indispensable to the survival of human communities.

First, religion suppressed anti-social behavior within communities by threatening community members with divine punishment – whether here or hereafter – in the absence of the law enforcement agencies that only emerged with the rise of agriculture and the eventual development of established city-states. The social cohesion of the more religious hunter-gatherer communities improved their chances of survival in the midst of an ever-threatening world.

Second, religion motivated community members to defend the community against external aggressors (with which the world was filled) not only out of the religiously induced sense of social solidarity but also in the religiously inspired belief in divine rewards for self-sacrifice in the interest of group survival.

The twin necessities for survival of willing cooperation within the social group and fierce competition among social groups may have made religion a powerful force in the evolution of the human species and, moreover, "explains why human nature is so contradictory, capable both of the most sickening cruelty and of the most self-denying care for others: the roots of altruism and of aggression are inextricably intertwined in evolutionary history."[iv] As they are, more specifically, in religious history.

The assumption that the biblical God is organically, that is, naturally, related to any religion is arguably questionable. The Hebrew title for "God" (*elohim*) was the plural form of the name of one of the primary Canaanite gods, *El*: "Though *elohim* can also be singular in Hebrew, its plural form may reflect the polytheism that preceded the monotheism associated with Yahweh, according to the biblical archaeologist William Dever."[v] The OT writers themselves vividly described the centuries-long conflict in Israel between monotheism and polytheism – characterized in terms of the worship of *Yahweh* versus the worship of idols. The exclusive worship of *Yahweh* only emerged after the return of Judah (the remnant of the southern kingdom of Israel from which comes the NT term "Jews") from Babylonian exile in the fifth century B.C.

Even the biblical term "God," then, was not original to the Bible. Instead, "God" is a rendering of the proper name of a Canaanite god (*El*), and was eventually adapted by the Israelites as a title for the voice who, according to their tradition, had identified itself to Moses as "I Am What I Am" (Exo. 3:14).[5] This formless voice – visible only in the forms of what the biblical writers called "angels" (literally, *messengers*), sometimes taking human form, sometimes other forms such as the burning-yet-unconsumed bush of the Moses story – came to be named *Yahweh* (possibly derived from the Hebrew word, *hayah*, for *to be*) and called *Elohim*, as the Hebrew rival to the Canaanite gods. According to the Israelite tradition, the voice had been heard by the patriarchs – Abraham, Isaac and Jacob – and, after identifying itself to Moses, continued to be heard by the prophets of Israel.

The term "God" represented the only *category of being* available to the Israelites for identifying the voice that, according to their tradition, seemed to have shaped their national destiny and had promised, through them, to shape the destiny of the nations. But their own prophets continually reminded them that their "God" was "holy," which was to say, *different* from the Canaanite gods and the gods of the other nations, and that they would have to learn to relate to their "God" in a radically different way.

The problem of theology – *God-talk*, from the Greek words for "God" (*theos*) and "word" (*logos*) – has been recognized by theologians as far back as the middle ages:

---

5   Or, alternatively, *I Will Be What I Will Be*, a rendering that adds an eschatological flavor to the name.

Whenever he made a statement about God, the theologian must realize that it was inescapably inadequate. When we contemplate God, we are thinking of what is beyond thought; when we speak of God, we are talking of what cannot be contained in words . . . . When reason was applied to faith, it must show that what we call "God" was beyond the grasp of the human mind. If it failed to do this, its statements about the divine would be idolatrous.[vi]

This idolatrous tendency to attempt to conceive of "God" as a being (with a capital "B") among beings was perfected in the modern era:

> The modern God—conceived as powerful creator, first cause, supernatural personality realistically understood and rationally demonstrable—is a recent phenomenon. It was born in a more optimistic era than our own and reflects the firm expectation that scientific rationality could bring the apparently inexplicable aspects of life under the control of reason. This God was indeed, as Feuerbach suggested, a projection of humanity at a time when human beings were achieving unprecedented control over their environment and thought they were about to solve the mysteries of the universe.[vii]

Modern theologians, of both liberal and conservative persuasions, adapted their understandings and explanations of God to the model of scientific rationalism, thinking "about God in the modern way, as an objective reality, 'out there,' that could be categorized like any other being."[viii] And so, the modern (as opposed to the biblical) notion of God as the Supreme Being, characterized by abstract terms like *omnipotence* and *omniscience* and *omnipresence*, simply made "God" out to be a super-human being, one without human limits.

Some theologians have argued that, to avoid idolatry, theology must identify God not as *a being* but *with being* itself: "We have no idea what being is: it is not – indeed it cannot be – an object of thought. We experience being merely as the medium through which we know individual beings, and this makes it very difficult for us to understand how God can be real."[ix] Which is to say that God is not a reality like other realities, which can be described and quantified so as to be integrated into a systematic worldview. Science, in fact, has shown that belief in God is not necessary to explain the natural world, making faith in the modern God seem increasingly at odds with science and, therefore for many, superfluous and irrelevant.

In fact, the biblical writers do not explain what God *is*. The name the voice gives to identify itself to Moses – "I Am What I Am" – amounts to the biblical writers saying, in effect, "God is what God is," whatever that may be, and nothing more can be said about what God *is*. They interpreted the featured events of their narratives as acts of *Yahweh*, the manifestation of *his word* (again, the voice) in the sense of being progressive fulfillments of the promise. While acts imply an actor, what the actor *does* does not necessarily reveal who or what the actor *is*.

The biblical God only and always comes to human awareness as a voice: "In the beginning was the word, and the word was with God, and the word was God" (John 1:1). To be sure, the voice of the biblical God came through beings, that is, angelic and human messengers, and has been preserved by beings, that is, the biblical writers. Nevertheless, the closest the biblical writers come to a definitive statement regarding God's *being* is in the fundamental confession of Israelite faith, attributed originally to Moses and echoed by the NT Jesus: "Hear, O Israel: The Lord our God, the Lord is one" (Deut. 6:4; Mark 12:29).

This biblically pronounced oneness of God may be interpreted as the claim that God is *a singular being* (a distinct problem for the doctrine of the Trinity) or that God is *the singularity of being itself* (a distinct problem for any attempt to formulate what God *is* in words). The problem with interpreting God's oneness in the former sense is that God then becomes one being among many, the virtual being without the limitations of a body but, nevertheless, so easily and compulsively reinvented in the image of humanity. The problem with interpreting God's oneness in the latter sense – in the sense of *being* itself – is that it raises the question of how *being* can reveal itself as a voice. Whose voice? Who is at the other end of the line?

The biblical answer is simply that the voice is God's, whomever or whatever "God" may be. And the voice is not a religious voice. The voice that speaks "the word of the cross" (1 Cor. 1:18) calls hearers *not* to a life of obedience to religious authority *but* to a life of freedom and responsibility. The time when religious authority figures and structures were necessary to frustrate human desire and regulate human behavior was the time of human immaturity. The path to "God" no longer leads through religious experiences governed by religious rules and accompanied by religious rituals. Which is to say that God used religion (in the form of the Mosaic law) for a time, the time of human immaturity, and has now discarded it not only because it is no longer necessary but also because it is an obstacle to human maturity.

Rather than concern themselves with what God *is* in-and-of-Godself, the biblical writers employed metaphors – which, as science continually illustrates, are as close as truth can come to unseen realities – like *King* and *Judge*, based on what the voice of their tradition claims to have done. The NT writers built on the metaphors of sovereignty and judgment but summed them up in the unexpected (at the time) metaphor of *Father*. Which is to say that whatever God *is*, and whatever forms his sovereignty and judgment may have taken in the time of human immaturity under law, the truth about God is that God loves all human beings *like* the very best of human fathers loves his children. And because he loves them, he wants them to grow up to function as free and responsible adults.

The religious search for God, then, is the human search for love: the love of oneself and of the other, in equal measure. It is the search not just for an authentic individuality to express and not just for an authentic community to belong to, but for authentic individuality-in-community. Rules and rituals were the scaffolding, which is necessary only until the building stands on a secure foundation. Which is to say that rules are only necessary until self-restraint becomes voluntary, until desire is suppressed or gratified in the interest of freedom and responsibility; rituals are only necessary until self-interest becomes unitary, until self-interest is identified with the whole of humanity. The biblical religion served its purpose of laying the foundation for human maturity, for individuality-in-community, for freedom and responsibility. Its time, then, came and went.

V

If the crucifixion of Jesus is understood as the end of the law and therefore of the religion, of the biblical God, then it can only mean that worshipers of the biblical God must embrace their spiritual status as *outlaws*.

Not, of course, as outlaws in the sense that they deliberately break civil or religious laws for private enrichment or to make a public statement. Rather, that they view *civil law* as a *necessary evil*: *necessary* to protect the rights of human beings from those who would exploit human beings for their own gain; *evil* because civil law must employ the infantile fear of punishment to modify human behavior, *and* because it inevitably becomes an instrument of the strong to oppress the weak. And Jesus-followers are outlaws because they regard *religious law* as rules for running spiritual nursery schools from which attendants are never allowed to graduate and enter the spiritual adulthood of freedom and responsibility.

The NT term for the informal association of Jesus-followers is the Greek word, *ekklesia*, rendered "church" in English NT versions. The linguistic origins of the English word "church" are not clear. What is clear from the NT data, however, is that "church" does not accurately translate *ekklesia*. While "church" is a religious word that applies to various levels of Christian organization – applying equally to an international institution ("the Church"), a national or trans-national denomination (like "the Southern Baptist Church"), or a local congregation (like "the Main Street Presbyterian Church") – *ekklesia* was a first-century term applying to any assembly of people, from a mob (see Acts 19:32) to a civic assembly (see Acts 19:39). The NT writers used *ekklesia* to refer to the informal gatherings of small numbers of Jesus-followers in one another's homes for mutual edification and the sharing of "love feasts" (Jude: 12), also called "the Lord's supper." It was not a religious word, and nothing in the word or in its NT use suggests the eventual institutional, denominational and congregational meanings of the word "church." Which is to say that "the Church" is a rhetorical invention of post-apostolic Christianity, with which Jesus-followers are certainly free to associate themselves, but to which, just as certainly, they are under no biblical obligation.

Believing "the word of the cross," then, does not mean aligning oneself with the religion called "Christianity" (a term not used by the NT writers). It does not mean believing that Christianity is the right religion to the exclusion of Judaism and Islam and all other religions.

Just as first-century Judaism came into conflict with Jesus and Paul because it had turned the Mosaic law into a religious system of condemnation, so the Christianity of subsequent centuries perpetuated that condemnation through its rejection of *spirit* in favor of *letter*. In so doing, in a matter of only a few centuries post-apostolic Christianity transformed itself from persecuted minority into persecuting majority via the fourth-century marriage of Church and State, a wedding performed by the Roman Emperor Constantine. This unholy union gave rise to centuries of Church-State sponsored violence and terror directed at pagans, Jews and Moslems, along with dissenters ("heretics") within the ranks of the Church. While the Enlightenment stripped Christianity of much of its political authority and, therefore, of its state-sponsored power to oppress the societies over which its lords had ruled, the Church (whether traditional Catholicism or the emergent Protestantism) continued to rule over its own faithful by means of the fear of divine retribution. Throughout its history (with a few notable exceptions) to the present day, Christianity has branded as illegal, religiously when it could no longer do so by means of civil law, the freedom and responsibility both endowed and enjoined by the biblical message.

While it may seem that contemporary Christianity has outgrown the excesses of its ecclesiastical history, the fruit born by its evangelical branches makes clear that it has not.[6] Evangelical Christianity is known in America for both what it is for and what it is against. Evangelical Christianity has virtually identified itself with the Republican political agenda (which is furthered by the passive or active compliance of the majority of Democrats): U.S. war-making in Iraq and Afghanistan in the name of "patriotism" (along with support for Israeli militarism, in the demonstrable interest not of the defense but of the expansion of Israeli lands); tax cuts, which demonstrably benefit only the wealthiest Americans, and the deregulation of industry in the name of "free trade" (a euphemism for the corporate greed manifested in the excesses of, among others, the banking, healthcare and oil industries, excesses finally exposed for all to see by the attempts at healthcare reform and the financial and environmental disasters of 2008 and after). Likewise, evangelical Christianity is known for its opposition to women's rights and gay rights, relying on the Republican party to uphold laws that prevent women and gays from being treated, in a civil sense, as the equals of men and heterosexuals, respectively. Whatever individual evangelicals may believe about the equality, or lack thereof, of women to men and gays to heterosexuals, the fact that they, collectively, align themselves with a legislative rather than a persuasive approach to addressing these issues, betrays their legal orientation to the God whose will they claim to be doing.

In terms of its support for American militarism around the globe, evangelical Christianity remains consistent with its worship of a "God"

---

[6]   Evangelical Christianity is, by a wide margin, the most vital and expansive branch of organized Christianity (with the exception, perhaps, of Mormonism). While most forms of Catholicism and liberal Protestantism have become little more than matters of social convention, evangelical Christianity continues to represent a potent social and political force that embodies the spirit of the law-god, for examples, in its attempt to employ the Bible as a standard of civil conduct, in its persecution of "sinners" both within and outside its ranks, and in its alignment with state-sponsored foreign and domestic violence.

whose legal demand of payment for sins found its satisfaction in the sadistic violence of crucifixion.

Christianity became a civil religion as soon as it wed itself to the Roman Empire (which had put Christianity's professed Savior to death) in the fourth century C.E. It had already prepared itself for that event by rejecting *spirit* in favor of *letter* very shortly after the passing of the apostolic generation. In contemporary America, evangelical Christianity battles to remain the civil religion of the U.S. in the face of increasing secularism and the rise not only of new-age spirituality but also of Islam.

But this has nothing to do with "the word of the cross" (1 Cor. 1:18). For to believe the message of "Jesus Christ and him crucified" (1 Cor. 2:2) is to abandon religion altogether for a life of freedom and responsibility. This is freedom from both the coercion of religious rules and threats and the compulsion of anti-social and self-destructive desires that religious rules and threats are believed necessary to restrain. (And freedom from the religious dues that must be paid to the churchly mediators between "God" and his worshipers in order to insure the continuation of the Christian religion itself.)

In sum, the NT Jesus died not because God needed him to do so for God to justifiably forgive sinners. If the NT claim that "God is love" is true, then neither human transgressions nor human shortcomings were ever a barrier to the biblical God's acceptance of human beings who sought to know him. And the biblical God could certainly have terminated his law, via prophetic announcement, without Jesus' having to be crucified. Why, then, as far as the NT writers were concerned, did the biblical God will, both by his permission and according to his purpose, his Messiah to be crucified?

Because only in so doing could the infantilizing, guilt-and-fear-instilling grip of law on the hearts of human beings be broken. Because only in so doing could the voice of God – "the word of the cross" – persuade human hearts that "God is love" and, therefore, calls his human creatures to a life of covenantal justice: the freedom and responsibility of love for themselves and for all of God's creatures.

Why the Death of Christ on the Cross according to Robert Hach

(Endnotes)

[i] Nicholas Wade, *The Faith Instinct* (New York: The Penguin Press, 2009), 15.

[ii] Ibid, 15.

iii Ibid, 12.
iv Ibid, 72.
v Ibid, 150.
vi Karen Armstrong, *The Case for God* (New York: Alfred A. Knopf, 2009), 141-2.
vii Ibid, 278.
viii Ibid, 287.
ix Ibid, 147.Epilogue

Miss the point of the Bible itself, 24,
The difference, p, 28

CPSIA information can be obtained at www.ICGtesting.com
233145LV00001B/78/P